CONTEXTUAL THEOLOGICAL INTERPRETATION

An Integrated Model for Reading the Bible

BO H. LIM

B
Baker Academic
a division of Baker Publishing Group
Grand Rapids, Michigan

© 2025 by Bo H. Lim

Published by Baker Academic
a division of Baker Publishing Group
Grand Rapids, Michigan
BakerAcademic.com

Printed in the United States of America

Library of Congress Cataloging-in-Publication Data
Names: Lim, Bo H. author
Title: Contextual theological interpretation : an integrated model for reading the Bible / Bo H. Lim.
Description: Grand Rapids, Michigan : Baker Academic, a division of Baker Publishing Group, [2025] | Includes bibliographical references and index.
Identifiers: LCCN 2025025382 | ISBN 9781540968890 paperback | ISBN 9781540969132 casebound | ISBN 9781493449880 ebook | ISBN 9781493449897 pdf
Subjects: LCSH: Bible—Hermeneutics
Classification: LCC BS476 .L54 2025 | DDC 220.601—dc23/eng/20250801
LC record available at https://lccn.loc.gov/2025025382

Cover design by Paula Gibson

Baker Publishing Group publications use paper produced from sustainable forestry practices and postconsumer waste whenever possible.

25 26 27 28 29 30 31   7 6 5 4 3 2 1

"How should Christians from diverse cultural backgrounds read the Bible well in today's world? What are the criteria for good interpretation that is both scholarly and contextual? Lim understands the issues well and maps the way ahead clearly, thoughtfully, and searchingly. An important book."

—**Walter Moberly**, Durham University (emeritus)

"An informed challenge for the usual practice of theological interpretation of Scripture (TIS) to embrace the important contributions of global voices. Expansive in its argumentation and irenic in tone, this volume aims to constructively move TIS in a more inclusive and thus more fully theological direction. There is much food for thought here, and incentives for fruitful conversation!"

—**M. Daniel Carroll R.** (**Rodas**), Wheaton College

"Old Testament scholar Bo Lim presents a sweeping and insightful assessment of the current landscape of biblical studies, examining its historical, cultural, political, and theological dimensions. Lim foregrounds the imperative of contextual theological interpretation as crucial to the church's ongoing mission. The study is both expansive and nuanced—expansive in its exploration of the historical trajectories that have culminated in contemporary approaches to theological interpretation and nuanced in its critical engagement with a range of models of contextual and theological hermeneutics. Lim ultimately advocates for an integrative model of biblical interpretation, one that is both theologically robust and contextually relevant, while remaining attentive to its inherent limitations. This is a much-welcomed resource in the field of biblical interpretation."

—**Chloe T. Sun**, Fuller Theological Seminary

"Bo Lim shows us what contextual theological interpretation looks like, where both words—*context* and *theology*—do work helping Christians faithfully interpret Scripture. Nothing Professor Lim teaches here promises we will always get it right. But following his lead will keep us honest, which—considering the violence we tend to do to Scripture, including the violence we do in the name of Scripture—means a great deal. Smart, wise, remarkably learned, and much needed."

—**Jonathan Tran**, Duke Divinity School

"A leading advocate for teaching students the significant role of multiple perspectives in biblical interpretation, Bo Lim takes readers on his historical quest—through the intertwining histories of theological interpretation and contextual interpretation—to claim an integrated hermeneutic of the Bible. Although scholars are not Lim's intended audience, any serious biblical studies student intrigued by the intersection of context, theology, and culture as essentials in the interpretive process will find this timely resource invaluable."

—**Emerson B. Powery**, Messiah University

"This volume wonderfully combines Bo Lim's broad and deep scholarship with his wisdom and passion as a teacher and minister. These virtues are all on display as he clearly and ardently argues for theological interpretation of Scripture to become more deeply engaged with and attentive to contextual hermeneutics. This book represents a real advance for theological interpreters of Scripture who want to serve the church."

—**Stephen Fowl**, Church Divinity School of the Pacific

"Many ministers and seminary students understand the importance of reading the Bible in ways that speak to the multicultural diversity of the church. They struggle, however, to integrate such readings with the historical, literary, and theological study of the Bible. These different approaches are often understood as distinct, with competing claims. In this book, Lim acts as a pastoral and scholarly guide to navigate the various assumptions, goals, and methods of contextual and theological biblical interpretation and to apply both approaches to the reading of the Bible. He helps Christians read the Bible not only for the sake of the church but also to engage the moral and ideological challenges to their faith and bear credible witness in the world. This is a book my students have been longing for, and I will definitely use it in my courses."

—**Janette H. Ok**, Fuller Theological Seminary

"Lim encourages us to take seriously a certain dissonance: The questions that biblical scholars typically ask are not usually the ones believers in the classroom and in the pew are asking. Involved in these questions is the recognition that contexts—both of authors and readers—matter for biblical and theological interpretation. Lim's latest volume can help scholars, teachers, and students resolve features of this dissonance for the sake of promoting a more attentive, critical, and reverent way of engaging the sacred texts and traditions of Christianity."

—**Daniel Castelo**, Center for Studies in the Wesleyan Tradition, Duke Divinity School

CONTENTS

PREFACE

The permanence associated with words in print makes authors fearful of publishing their thoughts since one's thinking always evolves. In this book I chronicle significant changes in the discipline of biblical studies, so no doubt this book will one day be outdated or in need of revision. Nevertheless, I write in the hope that these thoughts may help others navigate the present moment.

This book summarizes my thinking regarding the task of biblical interpretation over the past decade. It was born out of questions I, as well as my students, asked about how Christians ought to faithfully read the Bible in culturally diverse ministry contexts. I recognized a need for a pedagogical guide for reading the Bible in contextually appropriate and theologically sound ways. I do offer some reflections on pedagogy in the appendix of this volume, and I hope to write such a book in the near future, but this is not that book. I realized that before I turn to the pedagogy of interpretation, I first need to define the task of biblical interpretation. Even though this book is an academic work, it is not intended merely for a scholarly audience. Students use scholarship, so I wrote with them in mind, hoping they might make better sense of academic resources and discern what interpretive choices to make for their communities of faith.

I teach my students the necessity of interpreting the Bible in its ancient historical and literary context, *and* making use of the resources of the Christian tradition, *and* appreciating the contributions of readers from diverse contexts. There are resources that address each of these interpretive perspectives, but my students struggle with how to integrate them. My proposal for interpreting the Bible contextually and theologically is quite simple. It involves integrating the discourses of biblical studies, theology, and contextual interpretation. However, the actual task can be quite difficult because these disciplines have different assumptions and goals, make competing claims, and use an array of methodologies. This book attempts to understand and explain these varying discourses so that interpreters can make informed decisions. I have presented this material to students from diverse cultural backgrounds who have varying theological commitments, and they have applied its teaching in ways that suit their own contexts and concerns. My primary aim is to help Christians who hold evangelical and trinitarian beliefs minister effectively in culturally diverse North American contexts, but the book can also be helpful to those who possess different commitments or backgrounds than my own.

The book is divided into two parts: "Understanding Biblical Interpretation" (four chapters) and "An Integrated Model of Biblical Interpretation" (three chapters). The first chapter introduces what I consider the most pressing challenges facing contemporary readers of Scripture. Chapter 2 describes recent trends and developments in the field of biblical studies resulting from cultural changes in society and the church. Chapters 3 and 4 concern the rise of two disciplines: contextual biblical interpretation and its various forms (chap. 3) and theological interpretation (chap. 4). I describe the relationship of both disciplines to traditional biblical scholarship and identify what I consider to be their shortcomings. Part 2 begins with a model for biblical interpretation that identifies with an evangelical and trinitarian global Christianity that addresses the legacy of colonialism (chap. 5). Chapter 6 describes four different models of contextual and theological interpretation, and chapter 7 outlines my proposal that contextual and theological interpretation is a figural reading of the Scriptures according to one's cultural context and theological tradition. The book concludes with an appendix reflecting on the pedagogy for this approach.

It takes a village to publish a book, and lest I fail to acknowledge someone in particular, I will largely name groups rather than individuals. I want to thank Anna Gissing and the staff of Baker Academic for adopting and supporting this project. Much of this book was written during a sabbatical at Tyndale House, Cambridge, UK, and I am grateful for the support and friendship of the international group of scholars I met during my time there. My Wabash Peer mentoring group modeled excellent scholarship and offered encouragement, particularly during my sojourn in administration.

This book was written as my children transitioned into young adults, so they understand the commitment and sacrifices necessary for scholarship, and together with my wife Sarah they supported me in this project. Sarah and I cannot contain our joy and pride in who they have grown to be. My thinking on this topic has been stimulated by conversations with colleagues and students, so I dedicate this book to my colleagues in the School of Theology at Seattle Pacific University and the Seattle Pacific Seminary community, both past and present.

Seattle, WA
Christmas 2024

Part One

UNDERSTANDING BIBLICAL INTERPRETATION

1

The Strange Silence of the Bible in the Church

Half a century ago, James Smart wrote about the disappearance of the Bible in what he called *The Strange Silence of the Bible in the Church*. He observed that in the United States the Bible featured less in preaching, its use in educational ministries was declining, and biblical illiteracy was on the rise. Smart did not look very far to cast blame; he faulted his own peers in biblical scholarship and theological education for the Bible's demise. He believed the heart of the problem was a breakdown in communication. The seminary faculty was divided into multiple disciplines where they did not sufficiently communicate with one another, and collectively they failed to address the gap between the ancient context of the Bible and modern life. Smart described the work of the biblical scholar by saying, "The Biblical scholar determines scientifically the original meaning of the Scripture and then entrusts to others the difficult journey from the ancient to the modern world. Whether or not they reach the modern world without losing the precious meaning is not his responsibility. He need not consider it a function of his discipline that he should accompany them on their journey."[1] According to Smart, the gap between the Bible and contemporary life is *historical*. Because biblical

1. Smart, *Strange Silence*, 63.

scholarship failed to bridge this divide, the Bible became increasingly irrelevant. The modern world is the concern and responsibility of theologians and practical theologians, not biblical scholars. Biblical scholars concern themselves with the past. History is what divides biblical scholars from theologians, and it became the stumbling block that kept modern Christians from reading the Scriptures.

As a biblical scholar and pastor, I also have a growing unease about the "strange silence of the Bible in church" but for different reasons. Certainly historical challenges to interpreting the Bible persist. But what I increasingly observe is that the Bible's silence is largely due to ideological and moral reasons, and my concern is that biblical scholars and theologians fail to sufficiently address *these* issues because for so long our disciplines have fixated on historical issues.

I teach at a Christian college, so it is Christian young people—many of whom have grown up in the church—who are raising these challenges, not agnostics or atheists. Whether raised in conservative or liberal households, they all question God's justice when they read the Bible. In my introductory Bible courses, fewer of my students are concerned with age-old questions about whether biblical events actually occurred. Their primary objections to the Bible are moral and ethical. They have issues with the role of women in the Bible, the fate of non-Israelites, and divinely sanctioned violence. They object to the privilege and favoritism granted to Israel and God's elect servants in the biblical narratives, and they find the monotheistic claims of Scripture to be intolerant and potentially oppressive. Students acknowledge that the Bible is a source of great inspiration for many, has fueled liberation movements, *and* has been used as a tool of oppression. They are moved by the power of Scripture in Martin Luther King Jr.'s "I've Been to the Mountaintop" sermon to inspire a nonviolent civil rights movement. Yet they also have witnessed a US president pose for a photo op in front of a church with a Bible in hand after giving a speech on "law and order" in response to racial protests following the killing of George Floyd.

Christian discipleship today requires Christ's followers to read the Bible critically and as a sacred text, yet I well recognize these activities seem at odds. Is it possible to simultaneously exercise a hermeneutic of trust and a hermeneutic of suspicion, or will doing so create too much intellectual and existential dissonance? In our current culture wars, naivete and cynicism are incredibly alluring since they both provide the illusion of comfort and security. But neither should be mistaken for the path of Christian discipleship.

I also teach at a seminary where I observe similar trends. Some students enter seminary because they love Jesus and are drawn to ministries of justice and reconciliation, but they find that the Bible can problematize their theology and ethics. Some of them have seen people weaponize the Bible against their communities of color, so they view Scripture with suspicion. Moreover, they have taken cultural studies courses, so they cannot help but read the Bible with critical lenses. These students deeply value diversity and see its importance in theological education; yet they see that biblical scholarship is one of the least diverse theological disciplines, so they view it with suspicion or choose to ignore it altogether. Contextual biblical scholarship is an emerging discipline with varied and uneven resources, leaving students unsure about how to navigate them. Professors have diversified their reading lists, and they expose their students to multiple perspectives, but often students are left on their own to integrate nontraditional forms of scholarship theologically and ministerially.

Biblical scholarship is an industry[2] triangulating among educational, ecclesial, and publishing institutions. One need only to visit the annual conference of the Society of Biblical Literature to witness firsthand these operations at work. Yet currently the economic and numeric viability of all three of these institutions is precarious, and the academic discipline of biblical studies is experiencing tectonic shifts, changes on a scale not seen since the rise of historical criticism. Several recently published works propose new directions for biblical scholarship, such as David Janzen's *The Liberation of Method: The Ethics of Emancipatory Biblical Interpretation*. Janzen is concerned with the future of the academic discipline of biblical studies. My work differs from his by its focus on the role of the Bible in the church.

---

2. Todd Penner and Davina C. Lopez describe the current state of New Testament historical-critical scholarship as cultural production for capital gain in what they call "neoliberal subjectivity." See Penner and Lopez, *De-Introducing the New Testament*. In chaps. 3 and 5 I address how classic liberation theology served the "capitalist market of the theological production of goods." Althaus-Reid, "Disneyland," 42.

The tectonic shifts that concern me are not those of the academy; I am concerned about the massive demographic changes that have taken place in the church. While the church does not exist in a vacuum and therefore many of the concerns that Janzen raises also apply to the church, I write for different communities and for different concerns, so our proposals will inevitably differ.

Biblical scholars have long debated the question of whether biblical studies should serve the church or the academy. More often than not, the debate has taken place on Western soil that carries a legacy of Christendom and modernity. Finnish scholar Heikki Räisänen describes biblical scholarship: "Exegesis, as well as social sciences or medical science, can be pursued with the aim of providing people with means of coping with life—in this case, with their cultural and religious heritage."[3] The fact that he considers biblical study an acceptable "science" and part of the "cultural and religious heritage" reveals much about his sociocultural assumptions and context. Räisänen wonders why biblical scholars would choose to confine themselves to an ecclesial path when "the truly appropriate horizon today for biblical study (or any other discipline, for that matter) is humankind as a whole."[4] But what does one do when the culture is increasingly convinced that the Bible *is* the source of society's problems? Räisänen has a post-Christian pluralistic society in mind, but he does not address postcolonialism's critique of the legitimacy of biblical scholarship.

In an age of increasing polarization, I am sympathetic to Greg Carey's desire for what he calls an increase in "public biblical interpretation," and by no means do I think ecclesial interpretation should be done behind closed doors.[5] Yet Carey's proposal represents only a narrow slice of "the public," since his interlocutors are fellow academic biblical scholars who ignore or exclude biblical interpretations by multicultural ecclesial communities. Theological and ecclesial interpretation has been criticized for being insular, yet the irony is that biblical scholars are the ones who have openly questioned whether it belongs in the academy. The kind of ecclesial reading I am interested

3. Räisänen, *Beyond New Testament Theology*, 153.
4. Räisänen, *Beyond New Testament Theology*, 155.
5. Carey, *Public Biblical Interpretation*.

in does not call for fewer voices at the table but more. My ecclesiology is missional, so when I speak of ecclesial interpretation it assumes the important role of the Bible and the church in God's economy of salvation for the world. Reading the Bible for a missional church is, in Räisänen's words, for the sake of "humankind as a whole."

My theological and ecclesial commitments are trinitarian and missional, so the "multicultural church" I speak of includes communities that affirm the ecumenical creeds, the growing number of Christians of color in the West, and the rise of evangelical[6] and Pentecostal congregations in the Global South. I recognize many scholars involved in biblical studies, theological interpretation, and contextual interpretation do not have religious ties or ecclesial commitments. I certainly do not believe they ought to be excluded from the conversation, nor do I wish to insulate myself from any criticism they offer. While my theology is ecclesial, it is also public. To scholars who claim that the church has too heavy a hand in academic theology, I respond that the multicultural ecclesial communities I write for are often underrepresented and marginalized in the academy.

This book is written for both teachers and students of the Bible who wish to learn how to read and teach it for the ecclesial contexts I have described. It assumes readers have been influenced by academic scholarship and wish to engage it, so while I care about "ordinary readers," this book is not aimed at them. When I speak of the multicultural church, I refer to the church in my North American context as well as to the church global. By specifying North America, I do not suggest that this continent is more important than, or ought to set the agenda for, other regions. It is simply my attempt to identify the needs of my context and acknowledge the significant religious, social, cultural, and political differences among ecclesial communities that span seas and borders. Much of this book was written during a sabbatical in the United Kingdom, a country that shares much

---

6. I recognize that the term "evangelical" is hugely problematic in contemporary discourse, the literature on it is immense, and thorough engagement with it is well beyond the purposes of this book. I acknowledge that a third of evangelicals in the United States are persons of color who are a diverse group that do not fit the mold of white evangelicals. I write for these Christians as well as evangelicals globally who are also diverse and differ in substantive ways from white North American evangelicalism.

in common with the United States. Yet even there I was constantly reminded how differently my Asian race and US citizenship are perceived in another country and continent.

I consider the terminology "multicultural church" redundant, but I deliberately use it because often public discourse in the United States speaks of Christianity or theology only in reference to what is deemed normative for Euro-Americans. For example, historical, literary, and theological interpretation are not considered "contextual"; that label is reserved for interpretations such as womanist, African, and Native American. Another unhelpful title, "global interpretation," is also applied to these "contextual" interpretations. However, scholars use the term "global" to refer to different spheres, so it is important to determine what such language includes.[7] I will refer to "people of color" rather than using the expression "ethnic minority," and I will use the term "contextual" for practical purposes, recognizing that all such language has limitations. "Contextual" is especially problematic because it often assumes Eurocentric models where scholarship is legitimated by its ability to address the intellectual interests and cultural norms of white audiences.[8] Thankfully scholars of dominant cultures in North American have also begun to reflect on how their own social cultural location affects their scholarship.[9] Hopefully better terminology will someday prevail, but for now I will use "contextual" to refer to multicultural biblical interpretation.

I write from the perspective and interests of an Asian American Old Testament professor and ordained clergyperson teaching in a Christian liberal arts college and seminary in Seattle, Washington. I acknowledge my social location and institutional commitments from the outset because these contexts impact my scholarly interests. Global concerns are local concerns for metropolitan cities like Seattle, where large numbers of immigrants from the Global South and East have settled in the past several decades. My classrooms are very diverse and include students who are African, African American, Asian, Asian

7. "Global interpretation" will be discussed in chap. 5.
8. Goto, *Taking on Practical Theology*, 23–52.
9. See, e.g., Patte, "Male, European-American Critical Exegesis"; and Patte, "Male European-American Biblical Scholar."

American, Latino/a, Native American, Roman Catholic, Orthodox, Muslim, Buddhist, Sikh, nonreligious, queer, and undocumented.

While not all readers will share my particular context, my concerns align with the demographic changes in the church across the United States and around the world. For example, almost two-thirds of London's current population was born outside the United Kingdom, and 150 African churches were counted in New York City in 2011.[10] Half of what Wesley Granberg-Michaelson considers the ten challenges facing the church today directly deal with cultural diversity.[11] He observes that two-thirds of immigrants to the United States are Christians, who bring with them their cultural expressions of Christian faith. Denominations in the United States must embrace a nonwhite future. Fifty-five percent of all Protestants are evangelical and possess greater racial diversity than mainline traditions, while 40 percent of Catholics are Hispanic or Latino/a. Pentecostalism was the main contributor to the reshaping of Christianity from a predominantly Western to a non-Western phenomenon in the twentieth century. One out of four Christians in the world today is Pentecostal or charismatic; one out of four Pentecostals is Asian; and 80 percent of Christian conversations in Asia are to Pentecostal forms of Christianity. The present and future of the church in both the United States and around the world are increasingly nonwhite, non-Western, and Pentecostal or charismatic.

In this book I attempt to construct a biblical hermeneutic that considers four realities: (1) the lived experience of women and persons of color; (2) the hegemony of white persons; (3) the unique dynamics in Asian, African, and Latino/a Christianity; and (4) the explosive growth of evangelical and charismatic spiritualities. These are key areas of neglect within theological education in the United States.[12] Scholars have addressed these topics separately, but what does biblical interpretation look like when all of them are important? For example, scholars may address white hegemony *or* evangelical and charismatic

10. See Gornik, *Word Made Global*, 4.
11. Granberg-Michaelson, *Future Faith*.
12. See the series Theological Education Between the Times by Eerdmans. Several volumes are listed in chap. 2 under the heading "The Changing Face of the Church and Theological Education."

spiritualities, but rarely both. To address these concerns in isolation or separately ignores the hybridity of actual peoples. As noted above, a Pentecostal and charismatic faith was the main contributor to the growth of non-Western Christianity. One cannot address theology and ignore culture, and vice versa. Two of the concerns named are distinctly ecclesial (nos. 3 and 4) while two are not confined to the church (nos. 1 and 2); biblical interpretation must be attentive to the movements within the church and society, and it requires the use of theological and "nontheological" resources.

Not only am I personally committed to all four of these concerns, but they are also all represented in the students I teach. My commitment to all the above within a trinitarian framework determines which topics, methods, and conversation partners to engage and the values by which I make intellectual judgments. It is my baptism into the household of the triune God and my sense of calling to serve the multicultural church that determine and shape my understanding of the task of biblical interpretation.

Dale Martin researched the curriculum of ten divinity schools in the United States and concluded that Bible professors are failing church leaders in primarily three areas: (1) teaching students the theoretical tools to think critically about interpretation; (2) training students to think theologically about interpretation; and (3) helping students integrate the disciplines. He concludes, "The modern theological school, in far too many cases, is not doing a good job of teaching church leaders to interpret the Bible in creative, imaginative, and theologically sophisticated ways."[13] It is worth noting the things that Martin does not identify. He does not say that Bible students are lacking in historical or philological knowledge, nor that Bible professors fail to teach the technical skills of exegesis. The deficiencies Martin notes are in areas that fall outside the realm of traditional biblical studies. Christian ministry requires Bible preachers and teachers to interpret the Bible theologically for diverse contexts, and professors are failing at a conceptual level to train them for this task.

This book attempts to address the theological and theoretical concerns Martin raises. It contains a series of critical, theological, and

13. Martin, *Pedagogy of the Bible*, 28.

pastoral reflections on the task of reading and teaching the Bible for Christian ministry in diverse contexts. My commentary on the state of biblical scholarship is not directed at my academic peers per se. Instead, I try to explain the nature of the discipline for students preparing for ministry. The discussion may get technical at points, but this is necessary to expose students to the theory of interpretation, something Martin identified as currently lacking in seminary curricula. Before one conceives of a pedagogy of biblical interpretation, the task of biblical interpretation must be defined.

Several years ago I almost left my role as professor to pursue another career path. Biblical studies has always been a means for me, not an end. I chose to stay because I still believe that biblical studies can play an important role in Christian formation and ministry, and my concern is whether our writing and teaching as educators are effectively serving these ends. Much of the material in this book was presented in classes titled "Reading the Bible with the Global Church" and "Contextual Readings of the Old Testament." All to say, this book contains what I would like my students to know about the role the Bible should take in their lives and ministries and how they might use biblical scholarship effectively. Biblical interpretation for the sake of Christian ministry will demand more from readers than the discipline of biblical studies has offered in the past. If I as a biblical scholar wish to take seriously the lived experience of women and persons of color, the hegemony of white persons, the unique dynamics in Asian, African, and Latino/a Christianity, and the explosive growth of evangelical and charismatic spiritualities, I will need to reach beyond the traditional boundaries of my discipline and my social contexts. On one occasion when I shared some of these concerns in an academic setting, a fellow professor objected, "I'm an academic," implying that he felt constrained by the academy to stay within traditional disciplinary lanes. My students do not live according to the taxonomies of the academy and neither does the church, so while academics may have to navigate these difficulties, they ought not determine the hermeneutics for the global church.

The goal of this present work is somewhat modest since my thinking on this topic continues to evolve. The vital hermeneutical issues seem clear to me, but how to best address them is still a work in progress. Nevertheless, I have put these ideas in writing because I believe these issues need to be urgently addressed in theological education if we are preparing people for Christian ministry. I trust others will expand on these topics and improve on my proposals. I acknowledge my own disciplinary limitations so that while I address the field of biblical interpretation, my engagement with it favors Old Testament scholarship. I write so that readers might understand the current landscape of biblical interpretation, assess what opportunities and challenges they face, and effectively read the Bible for multicultural ecclesial contexts.

2

The Context of Biblical Studies as a Discipline

After the Collapse of History and the Text

In Ronald Clements's *A Century of Old Testament Study*, it is clear that in 1976, the year of the book's publication, the geographical and cultural center of Old Testament study was in northern Europe. The Germans Julius Wellhausen and Hermann Gunkel, the Scotsman William Robertson Smith, and the Norwegian Sigmund Mowinckel were its towering figures, and contributions of the American Brevard Childs were just beginning to emerge. Clements observes that early on "history was elevated to become the queen of the Old Testament sciences,"[1] and throughout the mid- to late twentieth century Old Testament studies vacillated between historical and religious interests. As Clements looked to the future, he assumed new methods would arise, but that history would remain the foundation upon which the

---

An earlier version of a portion of this chapter was previously published as "The Task of Reading the Bible for a Culturally Diverse North American Church" by Bo H. Lim, taken from *The Scripture and Hermeneutics Seminar: Retrospect and Prospect*, edited by Craig G. Bartholomew, David J. H. Beldman, Amber Bowen, and William Olhausen. Copyright © 2022 by Kirby Laing Centre for Public Theology in Cambridge. Used by permission of HarperCollins Christian Publishing. www.harpercollinschristian.com.

1. Clements, *Century of Old Testament Study*, 175.

discipline would be built. He writes, "What is overall of even greater importance is the awareness that there can be no going back to seek a return to some kind of theological, or hermeneutical, approach which ignores the demands of proper historical method. The roots of the Old Testament in real history reach down too far for this to be possible, and the vagaries of the older patterns of allegorical and typological interpretation which are to be found in abundance in patristic and mediaeval Christian exegesis can now command no confidence."[2]

Not only did Clements fail to predict the relegation of history's role in the discipline; he also was mistaken about the rise of theological interpretation and revival of interest in premodern readings of Scripture. Currently the amount of scholarship published on theological interpretation and Christian and Jewish premodern readings of Scripture may equal that of historical scholarship. Clements could not have known that biblical studies would undergo a transformation in the next several decades on a scale it had not experienced since the rise of historical criticism. Methodologies that had been normative for centuries would be challenged or relegated to obscurity, and the focus of study would dramatically change.

The title of Leo Perdue's 1994 book, *The Collapse of History: Reconstructing Old Testament Theology*, demonstrates that Clements was clearly mistaken. While historical concerns continued to remain important to Old Testament scholars, the years following Clements's work featured a movement away from history to text as text. The interest in semiotics was on the rise, so literary approaches dominate Old Testament theology in Perdue's *Collapse of History*. When he engages reader-oriented methodologies, the readers in mind are largely Euro-American. Perdue features feminist interpretation, and while he acknowledges liberation theology's roots in Latin America, Perdue focuses his attention on the Marxist interpretation of the US scholar Norman Gottwald. What is striking is that only a decade later Perdue published a reworking of his book, and while he maintains that historical studies had been decentered in Old Testament study, he has shifted his focus away

2. Clements, *Century of Old Testament Study*, 179.

from text to readers. The more recent work expands its concern for diverse and marginalized readers, and entire chapters are devoted to liberation theology and ethnic readings, feminist interpretation, mujerista and womanist theologies, Jewish readings, postmodernism, and postcolonial interpretation. These theologies, which Perdue labeles as "Radical Theology" in his 1994 work, were considered mainstream just ten years later. Gottwald is nowhere to be found, and instead the Latino Fernando Segovia and African American Vincent Wimbush are introduced as representative of liberation perspectives. The 2005 edition is not a revised version of the previous work; it is an altogether complete retelling of the trajectory of Old Testament theology.

Perdue's work focuses on Old Testament theology, and so it is not representative of the entire discipline of Old Testament studies. Nevertheless, the trends he observes pertain to biblical studies as a whole. After 2000, introductory works on biblical studies or interpretation almost uniformly added chapters on contextual interpretation in their revised editions. For example, the first edition of John H. Hayes and Carl R. Holladay's widely used *Biblical Exegesis: A Beginner's Handbook*, written in 1982, teaches interpretation entirely from a historical-critical perspective, beginning with textual criticism and ending with redaction criticism. By 2007, a third edition included a chapter titled "Exegesis with a Special Focus: Cultural, Economic, Ethnic, Gender, and Sexual Perspectives." Similarly the first edition of Michael Gorman's *Scripture: An Ecumenical Introduction to the Bible and Its Interpretation*, published in 2005, includes only one essay on "contextual" interpretation from an African American perspective. The 2017 revision adds the word *global* to its title and includes chapters devoted to African, African American, Latino/Latina, and Asian and Asian American forms of interpretation.[3] A 2016 introductory textbook not only strays from an exclusively historical approach by focusing on ecclesial interpretation but also includes a section on "Global Christianity" for each chapter.[4]

3. Gorman, *Scripture and Its Interpretation: A Global, Ecumenical Introduction to the Bible*.
4. Clifford et al., *Companion to the Old Testament*.

Biblical scholarship has begun to include diverse approaches, but the purpose for their inclusion varies or remains unclear. Are they for the sake of representation? Are they an alternative to traditional forms? Are they to challenge traditional scholarship? In such publications, "global" interpretation includes authors with vast differences in geography and culture, but it also includes Indigenous, liberationist, postcolonial, and other readings that are oftentimes at odds with one another. Used in this manner, *global* simply means non-Western, and it is a reminder that theological discourse remains Eurocentric.

Old Testament studies continues to attend primarily to historical and literary matters but has been giving more attention to diverse and marginalized readers. Clements was well aware that social, religious, and political contexts influence scholarship, so the recognition that cultural context impacts biblical study is not new. Significant scholarship on contextual interpretation has appeared since the 1970s, but the wider academy largely ignored it until the last two decades. The question that has most dramatically shaped biblical scholarship is not what is the Bible or how does one read it, but rather *who* reads the Bible. It is the changing face of the Bible's readers that has most dramatically impacted biblical scholarship. White male Germans, Brits, Norwegians, or Americans continue to be the majority in Old Testament study, but their *interests* no longer dominate the field. Those in the majority are realizing that they can no longer write solely for a Euro-American audience because the readership of the Bible has changed.

What catalyzed such drastic change in the nature of an entire discipline? One obvious factor is the explosive growth of Indigenous forms of Christianity in the Global South and East. Another factor is shifting culture in the West: its growing populations of persons of color and the increasing acceptance of diversity in education and society at large. Readers of the Bible are more diverse, the church globally is more diverse, and education stresses the importance of diverse cultures and disciplines. The push for diversity originates both inside and outside the church, and so when biblical interpretation is described as "contextual" or "global," a wide range of cultural contexts with varying and possibly competing interests may be in view. These contexts may be religious, theological, and ecclesial, but they may also be secular. They may be academic or popular readings of the Bible, or a combination of both. They might still employ traditional methods of biblical interpretation or reject them altogether. For some, diversity is to be celebrated, and for others it is a challenge or a threat.

The result is that the discipline is so diffuse that those interested in contextual biblical interpretation often find its resources confusing and inaccessible. Readers often do not know what they are to gain from such resources since they often do not fit within the genres of traditional scholarship. For example, one contextual reading may represent the views of someone who practices the exorcism of evil spirits, and another may present a critique of biblical patriarchy by an academic educated in Europe. Professors who recognize the importance of diverse perspectives are often at a loss in determining assignments and pedagogical outcomes. Students are unsure how representative scholarship is of the peoples it claims and how to constructively and critically engage it. This confusion often results in inaccurate caricatures of cultures and contextual interpretations that do not contribute to the ministry of congregations. Diversity is here to stay, but what is its purpose?

The Changing Face of the Church and Theological Education

Christianity's center of gravity has shifted from Europe and North America to Africa, Asia, and Latin America. As of 2018 the African continent contains the most Christians (631 million), followed by Latin America (601 million), Europe (571 million), Asia (388 million), North America (277 million), and Oceania (29 million).[5] White persons will soon be racial minorities in the United States, and similar demographic trends are occurring within US congregations. In response to these changes, models of theological education are undergoing significant rethinking and revisioning. Amos Yong observes, "If the 'browning' of the church across this continent involves not only its ongoing Latinization but also Africanization and Asianization,

5. Statistics are from the Center for the Study of Global Christianity at Gordon-Conwell Theological Seminary, https://www.gordonconwell.edu/center-for-global-christianity/resources/infographics/.

then the demands for theological education will stretch to include these contextual realities."[6]

Theological Education Between the Times is a series published by Eerdmans, and what is striking about it is that six of the ten volumes currently in print directly address the task of theological education in nonwhite contexts:

- Willie James Jennings reimagines theological education when it is not centered on the white self-sufficient male (*After Whiteness: An Education in Belonging*);
- Chloe T. Sun describes the history and contribution of a US seminary founded to serve the Chinese diaspora (*Attempt Great Things for God: Theological Education in Diaspora*);
- Amos Yong addresses the rise of evangelical and charismatic Christianity in the Global South and East and North America (*Renewing the Church by the Spirit: Theological Education After Pentecost*);
- Elizabeth Conde-Frazier narrates the diverse range of theological models and opportunities facing the Latinx church (*Atando Cabos: Latinx Contributions to Theological Education*);
- Keri Day testifies to her lived experience as a Black Pentecostal woman in predominantly white institutions (*Notes of a Native Daughter: Testifying in Theological Education*); and
- Maria Liu Wong recounts the formation of her own faith as a Chinese immigrant and her leadership role in founding a seminary to serve diverse urban communities (*On Becoming Wise Together: Leading and Learning in the City*).

What is noteworthy is that all these authors live and teach in the United States, not in the Global South or East, highlighting that these are concerns for the church in the West.

These issues and concerns have been raised in certain sectors of the church and academy for some time, but many Christians in the West considered them marginal. Mainline Protestants affiliated with

---

6. Yong, *Renewing the Church*, 28.

the ecumenical wing of the World Council of Churches have oriented their theology around postcolonial issues and have foregrounded interfaith, feminist, socioeconomic, political, and sexuality issues in their theology. For decades the academy has studied the Bible through the lens of liberation theologies, sociology, cultural and critical studies, literary criticism, postcolonialism, gender and sexuality, and race and ethnic studies. Since it has been half a century since the launch of the journal dedicated to such studies—*Semeia* in 1974—one cannot say that these ideological approaches are new. Trinitarian and evangelical Christian scholars have largely ignored these studies and approaches because they considered them incompatible with their theology and ministerial practice. For example, Anthony Thiselton acknowledges some of the contributions of reader-response theory yet adds, "But I am still doubtful whether a sufficient number of biblical scholars see that the Bible concerns engagement with the Other, and does not constitute primarily a mirror in which the wishes and desires of the self are bounced back, clothed with pseudo-divine authority."[7] He interprets the cessation of the journal *Semeia* in 2002 as the demise of these approaches, when in fact they have simply been absorbed into mainstream biblical studies.

In the United States, the culture wars involving race, gender, sexuality, immigration, the treatment of Indigenous populations, and anti-Muslim sentiment are waged in the church as well as the public square. Many pastors and church leaders have felt paralyzed engaging such matters, resulting in the perception of a church that is impotent or implicated. Many seminaries have responded to the racial crisis by mandating courses on racism. Day consequently observes, "Requiring courses in race/ethnicity demonstrates that race and racism are *theological* issues. . . . *What good is it to produce leaders for churches, social movements, and other faith communities who can interpret Barth or Tillich but cannot interpret their communities that are plagued by racial anger, frustration, and violence?*"[8] The current cultural crisis has led to a theological crisis, compelling Christian educators to rethink how to train clergy. Seminaries are requiring

7. Thiselton, "Future of Biblical Interpretation," 25.
8. Day, *Notes*, 53 (emphasis original).

reading lists to include works by women and people of color; calls to "decolonize" one's faith are coming from the mouths of evangelicals; and protests against the underrepresentation and mistreatment of faculty of color are occurring at seminaries and Christian colleges. Students of color and women are accusing white male faculty of reading the Bible "primarily [as] a mirror in which the wishes and desires of the [white male] self are bounced back, clothed with pseudo-divine authority." That is, the suspicion Thiselton projects toward reader-response biblical scholarship has been projected back toward its traditional forms.

Certainly one may view these cultural trends as faddish, ignore them, and choose to focus on traditional forms of theology and biblical interpretation. However, the inability of ministers to address issues of systemic injustice mars the church's public witness, and the continued growth of nonwhite Christians in the United States suggests that addressing ideological concerns will be a necessary aspect of Christian ministry. If the Bible is to bear on the life of a church intent on ministering to our changing times, its interpreters will need to be conversant with these issues.

Biblical Studies as a Eurocentric Discipline

For centuries, the definition of the discipline of biblical studies was obvious. Biblical studies was viewed as a linguistic and historical task aimed at understanding the ancient texts of the Old and New Testaments. Skills and knowledge required for biblical interpretation include facility with the languages of the Bible and comparative texts, textual criticism, various forms of historical criticism, ancient Near East and Greco-Roman backgrounds, and early Jewish and Christian studies. Within the Western academic tradition, biblical studies is a humanistic enterprise, and as such it is not only housed in seminaries and schools of religion or theology but also within colleges of arts and sciences. It is not uncommon for biblical studies professors to have their terminal degree in a discipline other than the Bible itself, such as in Egyptology or classics. Professors of the Bible might move between secular and religious universities because their research is not perceived to be ideologically driven. While some of these scholars populate seminaries and train clergy, others teach in departments of history, ancient Near Eastern studies, religious studies, or classics and so contribute to the liberal arts.

Because of Christianity's legacy in Europe and North America, the church and academy have continued to grant the Bible privileged status as both an icon in Western culture and a sacred Scripture for Jews and Christians. In a context where the Bible held religious, cultural, and political influence, biblical scholarship served multiple purposes with varied audiences. It nourished the spiritual life of the church, but it also directly or indirectly contributed to various non-religious functions. For example, Gregory Cuéllar observes how the archaeological scholarship of B. F. Westcott and S. R. Driver, based on the artifacts housed in the British Museum, advanced their careers but also helped establish the academic reputation of the British Museum, which in turn helped legitimate the colonial policies of the British Empire.[9] The recent opening of the supposedly nonsectarian Museum of the Bible in Washington, D.C., and the fact that the American Academy of Religion continues to hold joint meetings with the Society of Biblical Literature (SBL) both demonstrate the Bible's ongoing cultural influence in North American life. The Bible has held both sacred and secular roles, and therefore biblical studies has similarly served multiple functions.

When forms of biblical scholarship, particularly higher criticism, were perceived as a threat to the sacredness of the Scriptures, Christian and Jewish communities rejected academic study of the Bible and created sectarian scholarly societies, schools, and publications, many of which continue today. For example, several scholarly societies parallel SBL in programming but require all their participants to uphold specific doctrines. In more recent years SBL has wrestled with its own values to be inclusive in its approval of study groups that focus on religious forms of interpretation, such as Pentecostal, missional, and theological study groups. Some members of SBL argue that such forms of purportedly sectarian approaches ought to be rejected and SBL ought to maintain a sole focus on humanistic forms of interpretation, such as literary and historical analysis. The

9. Cuéllar, *Empire*, 127–211.

problem with this objection is that so many study groups with specific ideological commitments have been approved within SBL (e.g., feminist, Latino/a, postcolonial) that academic biblical study is no longer simply a linguistic, literary, and historical enterprise. While ideological approaches are not deemed a threat to biblical studies' academic integrity since they mirror the methods employed in other academic disciplines, theological approaches carry the potential for the discipline to be perceived as sectarian, insular, and uncritical. Yet in a pluralistic context, the lines between ideology, theology, confessionalism, and sectarianism are more difficult to draw. If SBL is going to accept ideological approaches, it must also accept theological ones. The end result is a fragmentation of biblical studies where identarian approaches have taken root. All these changes have led some scholars to celebrate the end of historical-criticism's hegemony, which in turn has ushered significant numbers of women and persons of color into the discipline. Other scholars lament the loss of common methodology and the splintering of the discipline into disparate interests. The SBL that for so long possessed significant unity because of its focus on a common text with a shared methodology now mirrors the pluralism and fragmentation of the American Academy of Religion.

The Impact of Interdisciplinary Approaches on Diverse Readings

Whereas historical interest dominated biblical scholarship in the twentieth century, its influence has certainly been curbed, to the point that its current role within the discipline is contested and its future standing remains to be seen. In addition to the diverse interpretive approaches Perdue described, there has been a proliferation of studies by scholars who do not read the Bible for its theology or its history. One need only look to the program units of the SBL to observe the vast array of topics and approaches to the study of the Bible. For example, some of the program units listed in the 2024 Annual Conference Program were Minoritized Criticism and Biblical Interpretation; Cognitive Science Approaches to the Biblical World; The Use, Influence, and Impact of the Bible; Bible and Film; and Biblical Literature and the Hermeneutics of Trauma. Admittedly the majority of program units still follow traditional categories, but it should be noted that they are defined largely by subject rather than method. So while at first glance the discipline may not seem much different than in the past, a quick read of session descriptions proves otherwise.

For much of the twentieth century, Christianity's prominent cultural influence in the West created a consensus among those inside and outside the church on the importance of the Bible. It was not difficult to establish biblical studies as a legitimate academic discipline. For biblical studies to maintain this standing, it had to meet the standards and interests of academic institutions in the manner of other disciplines. It was expected to display the attributes of all scholarship, so it needed to be open to public scrutiny and not be sectarian, and it needed to value innovation in its research. Legitimacy required that the discipline engage critical analysis, initially exercised with the same tools used in the disciplines of history, philology, literature, and textual criticism. Over time archaeology, anthropology, and philosophy would be included. In the West, where no one could dispute that the Bible was a cultural classic, universities offered courses on New Testament history and the Bible as literature, where students examined the Bible in the same way they would study Shakespeare or the writings of Josephus. In such an environment, fundamentalists, atheists, and others with competing ideologies shared scholarly standards and interests and held a common understanding of the discipline. While the sectarian Bible societies required members to hold specific doctrines, their methods of study did not significantly differ from those of mainline scholarship.

The university in the twentieth and twenty-first centuries has both contributed to and been affected by dramatic sociocultural changes. In the twentieth century scholars shifted their focus away from the historical, philological study of ancient texts to a plethora of other hermeneutical methods. Besides engaging newer literary methods, students read Homer through the lens of psychology or Shakespeare through the lens of postcolonial criticism. Some of these changes can be traced back to social movements and demographic shifts that took place on college campuses in the United States during the 1960s and 1970s. Michael Harris observes, "The student counterculture movement expanded student access and participation and the idea of what fields higher education should study. Enrollment among female and minority students continued to increase, as well as the need to include gender and ethnic studies as part of an expanding curriculum."[10] Diversity and the inclusion of marginalized perspectives in pedagogy, curricula, texts, faculty, and scholarship became a priority for all universities, academic societies, and academic publishers. Ethnic and cultural studies departments and scholarly societies formed and were inhabited by scholars from varying disciplines. These disciplines were forged within counterculture movements where the methodologies and ideologies of deconstruction, postcolonialism, and Marxism were prominent. Cultural competencies were expected of both students and faculty, offices of diversity were created, and traditional curriculum was questioned. The academy had to balance its long-standing pursuit of disciplinary expertise with increasing focus on diversity, equity, and inclusion. In literature, traditional methodologies and canons of study faced intense criticism and were replaced with Marxist, feminist, African American, and other forms of critical studies.

Harold Bloom, arguably the most influential literary critic of his generation, wrote a work defending the Western canon against what he called the "School of Resentment," an act that demonstrates that by the mid-90s these intellectual movements had become mainstream.[11] These changes were often initiated by student protests rather than by administrations, so more often than not institutions embraced the changes reluctantly. While conservative institutions have resisted these trends, increasingly they occur in Christian higher education, and especially in seminaries given the growing diversity of the church. But in recent years many places in the private and public sector have curtailed diversity initiatives, and public institutions in certain US states have even banned them, so their ongoing impact remains to be seen.

With the study of the Bible housed in the academy, it was inevitable that the same intellectual and cultural shifts across higher education would occur within biblical scholarship. The modern university is not only concerned about diverse populations but also interested in engagement between diverse disciplines. In interdisciplinary study, the Bible may not have a privileged place of authority,

10. Harris, *Understanding Institutional Diversity*, 32–33.
11. Bloom, *Western Canon*.

and the contemporary context of the reader may be considered just as important as the ancient context of the Bible. Biblical scholarship mirrors the topics, approaches, and interests in vogue in the wider academy, and therefore the Bible is studied from a nonreligious perspective for its nonreligious impact. For example, Fernando Segovia describes minority biblical criticism as the integration of "specific components from each field of study: from racial-ethnic studies, it foregrounds the set of formations and relations involving minority groups within a state; from biblical studies, it highlights the principles and practices of interpretation at work among critics from such minority groups."[12] He observes, "In this regard biblical criticism has by no means been an exception in the academy, but has followed the path of criticism in general."[13] Religion departments are often housed within a College of Arts and Sciences, so the context for reading the Bible may not be worship, prayer, and evangelism but rather political discourse, the arts, popular culture, and psychology. Postcolonial biblical interpretation researches how the Bible is used to extend the political, economic, and religious interests of hegemonic forces. Reception history, which traces the nonreligious impact of the Bible, has blossomed into a robust discipline. Both postcolonial interpretation and reception history have their own reference works, commentaries, monograph series, and journals. Scholars are cataloging the history of biblical interpretation in countries across the globe, and soon all peoples that have been impacted by the Bible may possess a heritage of biblical interpretation in their own culture.

Given that *who* reads the Bible most dramatically impacts biblical studies, contextual biblical scholarship will only increase as populations in the Global South and East outpace those of the north and west, migration and globalization continue, and cultural diversity expands in Western countries. With critical studies' increasing influence on the curriculum in Western universities, those who teach in this context may be required to be conversant with methods and disciplines traditionally considered outside the realm of biblical studies. Biblical studies has always involved ancillary disciplines such as ancient Near

12. Segovia, "Approaching Latino/a Biblical Criticism," 2.
13. Segovia, "Intercultural Bible Reading," 22.

Eastern studies, classics, Western literature, and Western philosophy, so interdisciplinary study is nothing new. What has changed are the disciplines of engagement, so that now biblical scholars read the Bible in conversation with William Blake and Charles Peirce as well as Toni Morrison and Franz Fanon. As long as universities and seminaries value diversity, biblical studies will need to address marginalized populations through the use of interdisciplinary methods.

The dominance of historical criticism in biblical scholarship meant that it often did not address the concerns of women and people of color. Scholars of color would not have been professionally rewarded for researching issues that pertained to their cultural contexts, so in order to succeed in the academy, they often adopted the methodologies and research interests of their Euro-American counterparts. It was not until the academy prioritized diversity in the past few decades that contextual biblical research proliferated. Unsurprisingly, many early forms of contextual biblical interpretation were written by scholars outside the field of biblical studies, and some of the works that would make the greatest impact occurred in grassroot movements. For example, the historian Justo González wrote one of the most popular works on Latino biblical interpretation, *Santa Biblia: The Bible Through Hispanic Eyes*, and base communities proved foundational for liberationist interpretation in Latin America and South Africa. Because biblical scholarship had long been defined by narrow interests and methods, its practitioners were not diverse, and it strove to maintain its standing as a legitimate discipline within the Western academy. Meanwhile scholars, both liberal and conservative, who practiced traditional forms of historical-critical scholarship lamented the loss of shared interests, methods, and goals within the discipline.

My narrative has largely focused on mainline institutions, but I should note that theologically conservative institutions have often been less willing to diversify. Their academic societies hold to more traditional categories of scholarship than SBL, and their faculty ranks are less diverse than their mainline counterparts. Conservative biblical scholars are typically less accepting of varying methodologies and diverse approaches since they often have less academic freedom at their institutions. Their conservatism may be motivated less out of a desire to maintain elite academic status than a concern that cultural diversity will invite heterodoxy.

Conclusion

Several important observations and conclusions can be drawn from this summary of recent developments in biblical studies. First, the discipline as a whole was resistant to diversity and changed only due to external pressures in education and the church. Second, since the Bible functions as both a secular and sacred text, its readers' motivations for seeking diversity in biblical interpretation may vary. Third, the field of contextual biblical interpretation, in addition to being a theological, ecclesial, and cultural movement, is also a political one. These observations are important to note when engaging in ecclesial contextual interpretation, and they generate the following conclusions about reading the Bible for the multicultural church:

1. It will require engaging resources outside the realm of traditional biblical studies.
2. Distinctions between which resources are sacred and secular, or "theological" and "nontheological," may not be clear.
3. Given the wide range of motives and goals for contextual interpretation, readers will have to discern what purposes biblical interpretation fulfills and what resources ought to be employed to achieve different aims.

3

The Need for *Theological* Contextual Interpretation

⟡

Mapping Contextual Interpretation: Liberationist and Intercultural

Contextual biblical scholarship is not new. For half a century it existed at the margins, and within the past twenty-five years or so it has been recognized by mainstream biblical scholarship. Its influence has certainly grown due to social trends in higher education, but its success is also due to the growth of the church in the Global South and East, the increasing diversity within the Western church, and the church's heightened concern for marginalized peoples. A new readership of the Bible was not satisfied with what biblical scholarship had to offer, and for some time their concerns were at the periphery, but that time is no longer. Because mainstream biblical scholarship has been Eurocentric, it naturally looked to European Christian interpreters or rabbinic scholars as its forebears, while the cross-cultural contexts of patristic interpreters were not sufficiently

An earlier version of a portion of this chapter previously appeared as "Reading in Context" by Bo H. Lim, taken from *The State of Old Testament Studies*, edited by H. H. Hardy II and M. Daniel Carroll R. Copyright © 2024. Used by permission of Baker Academic, a division of Baker Publishing Group.

explored. Missiologists have engaged biblical interpretation and theology in non-Western contexts for some time, but only recently has mainstream biblical and theological scholarship taken interest in their contributions.

Contextual interpretation is a massive, diverse, and even fragmented discipline, so any attempt to summarize it will inevitably be reductionistic and exclude important contributors. Most often the discipline's resources are categorized according to race, ethnicity, or geography, which has both merits and weaknesses. For example, within Black, Chinese, or Latin American interpretation are vast divergences in ideological and theological commitments such that the taxonomy may not be helpful and may even be misleading.[1] Similarly, any summary of white, Spanish, or North American interpretation would also fail to capture the diversity and provide meaningful coherence for those categories.

Based on my reading of the literature, I organize contextual interpretation into two categories: liberationist and intercultural.[2] These are not mutually exclusive categories, so they ought to be set in Venn diagrams rather than separate columns. They are distinguished by their different interpretive goals in or between various cultures. The goal of liberationist interpretation is ethical; it seeks to empower and advocate for marginalized peoples and decenter the power of hegemonic forces.[3] The goal of intercultural interpretation is educational; it aims for a greater understanding of the Bible across cultures and often involves attempting to preserve a common theology while translating the Bible into Indigenous forms. Communities in the Global South and East practice both liberationist and intercultural readings

1. E.g., Philip Jenkins excludes Latin American interpretation in his summary of biblical interpretation in the Global South and East because he finds it too diffuse to generalize. Jenkins, *New Faces of Christianity*, ix. I believe the same can be said certainly of Asian and possibly African interpretations too.

2. In Stephen Bevan's taxonomy of contextual theologies, his anthropological and praxis models would fall under liberationist, while his translation, synthetic, transcendental, and countercultural models would be intercultural. See Bevans, *Models of Contextual Theology*.

3. David Janzen proposes that due to the struggles of marginalized readers, biblical studies ought not to be judged on the basis of any method but rather on an ethic of liberation. See Janzen, *Liberation of Method*.

of the Bible. Both kinds of interpretation have important cultural and intellectual ties and influences with the West and have impacted mainstream biblical scholarship.

By the term "liberationist" I certainly include Latin American liberation theology, but also postcolonial, African and African American, Latino/a American, Asian and Asian American, Aboriginal, feminist, womanist, mujerista, queer, and other forms of interpretation that "see the Bible as a key resource in their emancipatory struggles."[4] It is these forms of interpretation that Leo Perdue views as the future of Old Testament theology and that largely dominate academic contextual biblical studies in North America and Europe.

The goal of intercultural interpretation is to gain greater insight into the Bible and other cultures through cross-cultural engagement and to read the Bible "through a particular *conceptual frame of reference* derived from the worldview and sociocultural context of a particular cultural community."[5] It is certainly not at odds with the goals of liberation, but it may not prioritize these goals in the same manner. This form of interpretation is found in missiology, intercultural studies, world Christianity or majority world theology, non-Western Christian scholarship, and missional hermeneutics. Henning Wrogemann subsumes mission studies under the broader "intercultural theology and hermeneutics" since the latter studies Christianity in areas of growth and decline, engages nontheological issues, and is concerned for intercultural ecumenism.[6] Intercultural interpretation also includes African and African American, Latino/a and Latino/a American, Asian and Asian American, female perspectives, and others in many of the same categories as the liberationist models, with the exception of those theologies that are considered incompatible with its interests. Not surprisingly, this form of interpretation is found more within ecclesial bodies and may not impact the academy in the West to the same extent as liberationist interpretation. Scholars may write for both liberationist and intercultural purposes, so the goals are interrelated and certainly not mutually exclusive. Intercultural education may empower communities for

---

4. Janzen, *Liberation of Method*, 2.
5. Ukpong, "Inculturation Hermeneutics," 27 (emphasis original).
6. Wrogemann, *Intercultural Theology*, 15–27.

liberation, and both forms of study may aim to decenter traditional forms of biblical scholarship.

Liberationist interpretations are united in their shared struggle against injustice and the oppression of the poor and marginalized. They may share many characteristics, but their methodologies and foci vary depending on the needs and concerns of particular sociocultural groups. In this mode of reading as much attention is given to the reader's sociocultural background as to that of the biblical text. Texts are never understood in abstraction, and the contexts of readers are similarly examined. Fernando Segovia writes:

> I believe that the time has come to introduce the real reader, the flesh-and-blood reader, fully and explicitly, into the theory and practice of biblical criticism; to acknowledge that no reading, informed or uninformed, takes place in a social vacuum or desert; to allow fully for contextualization, for culture and experience, not only with regard to texts but also with regard to readers of texts, with a view of all readings as constructs proceeding from, dependent upon, and addressing a particular social location, however circumscribed.[7]

Segovia's proposal is nothing short of a redefinition and reorientation of the discipline of biblical studies. It means that sociology, psychology, cultural studies, gender studies, postcolonial studies, ethnic studies, and other disciplines would not be applied only to the study of the Bible, but they would also be used to understand authors, readers, and interpretive traditions. The *Ideologiekritik* of the Marxist Antonio Gramsci undergirds the method of many liberationist scholars: "The starting-point of critical elaboration is the consciousness of what one really is, and is 'knowing thyself' as a product of the historical process to date, which has deposited in you an infinity of traces, without leaving an inventory."[8] The interpretive task of the liberationist scholar is to catalog and expose this "infinity of traces," and critical studies are required tools for excavation because, as Gramsci observes, they were deposited "without leaving an inventory." While these scholars are often concerned with

---

7. Segovia, "Hermeneutics of Diaspora," 57.
8. Gramsci, *Selections*, 324, as quoted in Carroll, "An Infinity of Traces," 25.

Indigenous forms of religion and native sociocultural issues, they acquired their hermeneutical tools in the Western academy. Many liberationist scholars received their academic training in Europe; rather than being grassroots theologians, they are what R. S. Sugirtharajah describes as "transplanted or uprooted professionals who return to their community after learning their craft and Western theories of oppression."[9]

Liberationist interpreters fall on a continuum between those who criticize the Bible for its oppressive ideologies to those who believe that the message of liberation is intrinsic to the Bible. One need only to remember Jesus's repeated warnings to "beware of the yeast of the Pharisees" (Mark 8:15) to recognize that resisting oppressive readings of Scripture is an act of discipleship. The oft-cited words of Nancy Ambrose, the grandmother of civil rights leader Howard Thurman, demonstrate the need for marginalized groups to critically appropriate biblical teaching:

> "During the days of slavery," she said, "the master's minister would occasionally hold services for the slaves. Old man McGhee was so mean that he would not let a Negro minister preach to his slaves. Always the white minister used as his text something from Paul. At least three or four times a year he used as a text: 'Slaves, be obedient to them that are your masters, as unto Christ.' Then he would go on to show how it was God's will that we were slaves, and how, if we were good and happy slaves, God would bless us. I promised my Maker that if I ever learned to read and if freedom ever came, I would not read that part of the Bible."[10]

This quote demonstrates that even for those who have been oppressed by the words of the Bible, it continues to hold a special significance or authority. For example, the *Dalit Bible Commentary* is based on the correspondence between the "Two Narratives: Judeo-Christian and Indic Enslavement and Liberation," but it also asks, "How is it that interpreters practitioners and propagators of Christian Scripture in India engaged in their task, without confronting the caste system and

9. Sugirtharajah, *Asian Biblical Hermeneutics*, 129.
10. Thurman, *Jesus and the Disinherited*, 31.

its practice in India, though they were aware of the slavery-liberation story in the Bible?"[11] Liberationist scholars observe that among the poor and marginalized the Bible remains one of the few accessible resources for social change. If the Bible is respected across all strata of society, liberative readings of the Bible offer the poor and marginalized a resource when they have few other options. Since liberation is the goal of Bible reading, texts focused on the exodus and the exile have often been used, while texts such as the conquest narratives and the anti-miscegenation teachings of Ezra-Nehemiah are critiqued for their oppressive teachings.

Liberationist scholars are aware that revolutionary movements can lead to new regimes that go on to equally, or more ruthlessly, oppress people. In order to mitigate this possibility, many scholars identify themselves as "organic intellectuals"[12] in the manner described by Gramsci; they seek solidarity with marginalized peoples by reading the Bible with them so that their scholarship reflects the concerns and interpretations of the oppressed rather than of elite intellectuals. Liberationist interpreters find a model in the dialogical method of reading the Bible with the poor captured in *Love in Practice: The Gospel in Solentiname* by the Nicaraguan priest Ernesto Cardenal. Other influential forms are African American slave narratives, which demonstrate how Black slaves, through reading the very Bible of their colonial masters, resisted their oppression and fueled their own emancipation.[13] Bible studies among base communities proliferated, and institutes for the study of the Bible among the poor were established in Brazil and South Africa. These institutes were intended to educate and empower poor communities where academics did not teach per se, but rather they facilitated study of the Bible so that interpretation was an act of the people. In this form of contextual study, the interpretations of "ordinary readers" and not biblical scholars comprise scholarship.[14] Typically this form of interpretation occurs more in the Global South and East, and even though most scholars in Europe and North America may not be facilitating Bible studies among base

11. John, "Two Narratives," xxiii.
12. Gramsci, *Selections*, 9.
13. Powery and Sadler, *Genesis of Liberation*.
14. See, e.g., G. West, *Reading Other-Wise*.

communities, many still consider solidarity with marginalized people as vital to their hermeneutic. For example, the womanist scholar Renita Weems states, "Like feminist biblical hermeneutics, womanist biblical hermeneutical reflections do not begin with the Bible. Rather, womanist hermeneutics of liberation begin with African American women's will to survive as human beings and as the female half of a race of people who live a threatened existence within North American borders."[15]

While liberationist readings often include extensive critiques of historical criticism, many of them continue to use historical-critical tools such as source criticism, form criticism, and rhetorical criticism. What unites liberationist interpretation is its critique of hegemony, and since historical criticism and its claim for objectivity were used to marginalize non-Euro-American and non-male voices, very often historical criticism and other traditional forms of theology are its targets. For example, in principle David Janzen has no objection to a belief in the divine inspiration of Scripture. What he objects to is the practical use of this doctrine by those in positions of power:

> This is part of his [Anthony Thiselton's] argument that religious doctrine could not be reliable unless there is some aspect of meaning to scripture that humans do not produce, and my concern with this sort of objection to understanding the meaning of biblical texts as a human production is that it might lead some to settle on a particular reading of a text, one promoted by the more socioeconomically privileged readers who tend to wield interpretive power, and then to divinize it, taking a limited human understanding to be the equivalent of omniscient divine intention that no one should ever challenge.[16]

Here Janzen expresses his suspicion of historical and theological claims based on Scripture, particularly by those who have traditionally held positions of power.

---

15. Weems, "Re-Reading for Liberation," 24.
16. Janzen, *Liberation of Method*, 17. Angela Parker writes an extensive critique of how inerrancy can serve white supremacist interests. See Parker, *If God Still Breathes*.

At this point I will distinguish between two categories of what I have called liberationist interpretation: liberation hermeneutics and postcolonial criticism. Both of these forms of biblical interpretation seek the emancipation of marginalized peoples from oppressive forces. They both critique the ways those in power have weaponized the Bible against the interests of the poor. Yet they differ on whether the Bible should continue to be a normative resource for the marginalized in their liberative struggles. Traditional Latin American and South African liberation theologians largely assumed a normative Catholic faith or Christian spirituality, where the Bible carries special significance because of its divine origins. According to the Latin American liberation theologians Leonardo Boff and Clodovis Boff, "The liberation theologian goes to the scriptures bearing the whole weight of the problems, sorrows, and hopes for the poor, seeking light and inspiration from the divine word."[17] Given this, it is no wonder that many North American Christians in mainline and progressive evangelical traditions have embraced liberation theology since it aligns with their views of the Bible and social ethics.

Sugirtharajah, the most prolific postcolonial biblical critic, describes the areas of convergence and divergence between liberation and postcolonial hermeneutics in his work *Postcolonialism Criticism and Biblical Interpretation*. He says they possess genealogical ties within biblical studies, with liberation hermeneutics preceding postcolonial hermeneutics. Liberation hermeneutics is characterized by its commitment to eradicate poverty, affirm liberation as a singular reality that encompasses both the sacred/secular and individual/communitarian spheres, privilege the perspective of the poor, and abhor neutrality. This last feature is evident in the way liberation theologians devised the notions of a "hermeneutical circle" and "hermeneutics of suspicion."[18]

Sugirtharajah says liberation hermeneutics developed in three phases: (1) classic liberation hermeneutics or Latin American liberation theology that engages in a discourse of universal liberation; (2) the people's reading, where Bible reading occurs at the grassroots

17. Boff and Boff, *Introducing Liberation Theology*, 32.
18. Sugirtharajah, *Postcolonial Criticism*, 105–6.

level in base Christian communities by nontrained readers; and (3) identity-specific reading, where liberation theology is now a series of genres engaged by a plurality of minority voices.[19] At present all three forms continue to be practiced, with the third being the most influential.

Given the liberation hermeneutic's opposition to hegemony, it was inevitable that a hermeneutic of suspicion would find interpretations of the Bible, as well as the Bible itself, problematic. Sugirtharajah writes, "What postcolonialism attempts to do is to demonstrate that the Bible itself is part of the conundrum rather than a panacea for all the ills of the postmodern/postcolonial world."[20] In his seminal study of liberation hermeneutics, Gerald West compares the biblical hermeneutics of two antiapartheid activists: Allan Boesak, who considers the message of liberation within the text of the Bible, and Itumeleng Mosala, who views the Bible as a source of oppression and seeks to relocate the ethics of Black liberation outside biblical teaching.[21] Postcolonial biblical criticism places colonialism at the center of biblical scholarship, and its aim is to liberate people from narratives imposed on them and totalizing narratives in particular. It is completely a deconstructive enterprise and does not possess methodological tools of its own. Instead, it employs existing methods as "as counter-tools in an act of disobedience against the text and its interpretation."[22] To borrow a legal metaphor, postcolonial criticism does not attempt to build a legal case; it tries to establish reasonable doubt in others. Sugirtharajah summarizes the goal of postcolonial hermeneutics: "The purpose is to interrupt the illusion of the Bible being the provider of all answers, and to propose new angles, alternative directions, and interjections which will always have victims and their plight as the foremost concern."[23]

Postcolonial criticism is not opposed to the Bible in principle or to theologies of liberation that appeal to the Bible for support. Sugirtharajah recognizes that the Bible empowers marginalized people, and he does

---

19. Sugirtharajah, *Postcolonial Criticism*, 104–5.
20. Sugirtharajah, *Postcolonial Criticism*, 100.
21. G. West, *Biblical Hermeneutics of Liberation*, 42–62.
22. Sugirtharajah, *Postcolonial Criticism*, 99.
23. Sugirtharajah, *Postcolonial Criticism*, 102.

not want to disenfranchise them from using this resource. He wants to remind them that the interpretations they use to seek their emancipation, if left unchecked, carry the potential to oppress others. He writes, "It is important to be mindful that this same Bible contains elements of bondage and disenfranchisement. What postcolonial biblical criticism does is to make this ambivalence and paradox clear and visible."[24]

Sugirtharajah opposes conservative Christians and liberation theologians who proclaim the totalizing narratives that salvation is found exclusively in Jesus Christ or that God is always on the side of the poor, but he also resists liberal Christianity for mollifying the violence in the Bible in its attempt to derive universal ethical principles from it. Yet even Sugirtharajah, a champion for diverse readings of the Bible, is concerned that "while identity hermeneutics has allowed people to empathize with social movements which try to rectify the injustices of the past, the obsessive focus on narrow identity issues may result in the neglect of shared values. . . . One needs to be alert to the likely adverse consequences of the splintering of marginal hermeneutics. It is unlikely that such a fragmented status will radically trouble mainstream biblical study."[25] Sugirtharajah's comment reveals what many Christian scholars suspect: The motive behind diverse and contextual readings is to decenter mainstream scholarship from its privileged status. Sugirtharajah acknowledges that identity politics animate and motivate these readings; yet he also laments that if they are taken too far the coalition will splinter and their political influence will evaporate. This is consistent with his claim that postcolonial biblical interpretation places colonialism instead of the Bible at the center of biblical study. Sugirtharajah's interest in the Bible is solely for the purposes of decentering hegemonic forces, and therefore he worries too much diversity might hurt this cause.

Evaluating Liberation and Postcolonial Hermeneutics: The Limits of Liberation

Liberationist interpretation pragmatically uses texts that uplift and empower the poor and marginalized to advocate for social change.

24. Sugirtharajah, *Postcolonial Criticism*, 101.
25. Sugirtharajah, "Muddling Along," 11, as quoted in Moore and Sherwood, *Invention*, 120.

One cannot deny the powerful effect of biblical narratives in particular on liberative movements throughout history. In liberation hermeneutics, the role of the Bible is subordinated within a program of liberation of the poor. Biblical interpretations, interpreters, and even texts that contribute to the oppression or neglect of the poor are to be rejected. Because its concerns are social and political, liberation hermeneutics is concerned with the public use of the Bible. It repurposes a tool that colonial masters weaponized against the poor as a countermeasure to empower the marginalized. Cornel West sums up tensions in liberation theology: "Christianity and Marxism are the most vulgarized, distorted traditions in the modern world, yet I believe the alliance of prophetic Christianity and progressive Marxism provides a last humane hope for humankind."[26]

Because liberationist interpretation rejects traditional academic methods, scholars fear that accepting this form of interpretation will jeopardize biblical scholarship's academic credibility and integrity as a discipline. Robert Carroll candidly states, "In my opinion, ideological readings of the Bible are lazy readings."[27] Initially classic liberation theology's most strident critics were the Roman Catholic Church and conversative Protestant theologians, but in recent years postcolonial theologians have accused liberation theologians of being uncritical fundamentalists or exploitative capitalists. Some perceive that liberation theologians do not represent the interests of the marginalized but rather the agenda of elite intellectuals who capitalize on the plight of the poor. Marcella Althaus-Reid, a postcolonial critic who participated in liberation movements in Argentina in the 1980s, writes a scathing critique of classic and popular liberation theologians, accusing them of constructing an artificial theology of the poor to serve the interests of North American and European academics. She explains the title of her article, "Gustavo Gutiérrez Goes to Disneyland: Theme Park Theologies and the Diaspora of the Discourse of the Popular Theologian in Liberation Theology," by saying, "Liberation Theologies as theme parks function at the level of popular attractions and have done a lot for the book market of

---

26. C. West, *Prophesy Deliverance*, 95, as quoted in Tran, *Asian Americans*, 24.
27. Carroll, "An Infinity of Traces," 34.

the Western world, as an extension of the capitalist market of theological production of goods."[28] She argues that liberation theology's
narratives of a "theology of the poor" and efforts to write a liberation systematic theology demonstrate that it is merely an adaptation
of Western Christian theology that serves the academic "touristic
theological industry." She argues that in reality "liberation theology
in action has always been diasporic and unsettled, more in tune with
Chaos Theory than with North Atlantic systematic theology."[29] It
essentializes the poor in its descriptions and depictions such that
"one may think that the poor in Latin America use uniforms, speak
the same language, have the same beliefs, and look the same."[30] She
says liberation theology's so-called grassroots Bible study practices
of reading with "ordinary readers" mask the fact that elite academics
actually directed and edited the conversations. Claims of normative
Bible study practices in Base Ecclesial Communities (BECs) misrepresented the truth since the participants were largely illiterate, and
"this meant that the Bible was, at times, read as an oracle to divine
the future, a talisman for good luck, an allegory or a literal truth.
The allegorical form was approved by European academia, while the
literalist forms were ignored."[31] For Althaus-Reid, the result is that
liberation theologians created a "Disneyland" and achieved success
in the Western academy, while the real poor have been excluded in
the globalization process and now refuse to support BECs and their
Bible studies.

28. Althaus-Reid, "Disneyland," 42.
29. Althaus-Reid, "Disneyland," 53.
30. Althaus-Reid, "Disneyland," 40n3.
31. Althaus-Reid, "Disneyland," 49–50. Brian Blount describes an instance where
Ernesto Cardenal recognizes that his peasant audience's perspective is at odds with
Jesus's statements about the poor in Matt. 26:6–13, so Cardenal reinterprets the
passage to mean "there will always be poor people as long as Jesus isn't there. But
when there's only equality and justice, and no needy, no beggars, Jesus will be with us
again." Cardenal, *Love in Practice*, 4:98, as quoted in Blount, *Cultural Interpretation*,
43–44. Blount writes, "Here is a good example where the interpretative conclusions
are forcibly molded to fit the sociolinguistic needs of the community. Textual and
ideational controls have been overridden in favor of interpersonal demands. Instead
of moving beyond the boundaries, the peasants in this case have destroyed them.
The result is an inadequate and problematic interpretative conclusion." *Cultural
Interpretation*, 44.

Some biblical scholars may chafe when reading postcolonial critics, yet I often find their honesty refreshing. For example, Sugirtharajah is an equal opportunity critic, consistently applying his ideological commitments to his methodology and interpretive practices in a way that exposes the inconsistencies of both conservatives and liberals. He exposes the myth that people in the West can "decolonize" their theology. Sugirtharajah observes that when people try to reject Western concepts in favor of Indigenous ideas or "ordinary readings," the result is more often a modern and Western construction, since their so-called decolonial practices are mediated by academics who have been educated in the West for the purpose of decentering hegemony. Sugirtharajah does not object to contextual theologies in themselves but rather to the false premise that modern reconstructions of Indigenous theologies are free of colonial influences. For example, he notes that Indian attempts at indigenization through the recovery of the Sanskrit tradition resulted in Indians participating in their own orientalizing. He writes, "We realized that our efforts to create an India of our dreams, as a reaction to the continual threat of the universalizing nature of Western theories, divorced us from current reality and history, and in a way worked against our own people. . . . Paradoxically, the use of an indigenous method ended up being condemned as elitist, oppressive, and alienating."[32]

When contextual theologies make universal claims, or erase or rewrite other traditions in the process of recovering their own, they mimic their colonial masters through their use of totalizing narratives. For example, Israel Kamudzandu argues that just as Paul transformed the dominant "imperial" ancestry of his day with the ancestry of the Jews in Romans 4:1–25, postcolonial Christians ought to reconstruct their own spiritual genealogies by incorporating their own cultural heroes as spiritual ancestors.[33] In response, Renie Choy concludes, "I daresay some may find this reading not only *not* postcolonial but fundamentally colonial,"[34] since in keeping with Willie Jennings's argument in *The Christian Imagination*, "supersessionist

32. Sugirtharajah, *Asian Biblical Hermeneutics*, 131–32.
33. Kamudzandu, *Abraham as Spiritual Ancestor*.
34. Choy, *Ancestral Feeling*, 58 (emphasis original).

readings of any sort—either ones which displace Israel within the
economy of salvation or, as in Kamudzandu's work, ones that re-
interpret Abraham as the forebearer of all people of faith—rely on the
same colonizing logic."[35] Kamudzandu's interpretation likely lacks
the social and political means to oppress others in the same manner
European colonizing logics have done. Nonetheless, it is a reminder
that what may portray itself as liberation or postcolonial theology
can operate with the same methodology it critiques.

Conclusion

Should liberation be the primary criteria by which biblical interpretation is measured, as recently argued by Janzen?[36] I wonder if
such a hermeneutical strategy may lead to even less engagement with
the Bible in the United States. The two most recent progressive liberative movements in the United States to bring about significant
social change, Blacks Lives Matter and Me Too, were nonreligious
movements. Yes, Christians participated in these movements and
may have provided a biblical and theological rationale for doing so,
but the Bible was not instrumental in either of them. Instead, many
perceive the Bible as a means of suppressing liberative movements
such as LGBTQ+ inclusion and abortion rights. Certainly progressive Christians can make a case that the Bible supports such causes,
but the arguments are often complex and nuanced so that activists
lose patience with the Bible and find it more expedient to reject it
altogether. Effective biblical interpretation for liberation occurs in
cultures where marginalized populations hold the Bible in high regard, but that seems to be diminishing in the United States, even
among communities of color.

I have presented the Bible as a liberative text to my students, particularly those who are atheists, but many of them remain unper-
suaded. They find liberation an insufficient reason to read the Bible
since it often problematizes liberation rather than contributes to it.
They can look for texts less publicly disputed than the Bible to inspire

---

35. Choy, *Ancestral Feeling*, 58.
36. Janzen, *Liberation of Method.*

and inform them for liberative causes. They believe it is precisely an ecclesial and societal fixation on the Bible that is the cause of oppressive ideologies and practices. They have moved beyond liberation to embrace the postcolonial critique that marginalized peoples would be better off without the Bible. I well recognize this is not the same case around the world. The United States is an affluent country, so the progressive liberative causes here tend to focus on race, gender, and sexuality rather than an issue like poverty where the Bible can make a clearer contribution.

By no means am I suggesting there is a "collapse of liberation" in the same manner Perdue describes a "collapse of history" in biblical interpretation. But it does seem that postcolonial critics have rightly identified the limitations of liberation, and my classroom experience confirms for me that this is true. But if the Bible is not to be primarily interpreted for history or liberation, what then is the goal of biblical studies? I believe the Bible is to be interpreted as a sacred text for the global church to commune with God and live out its redemptive witness in the world. I believe the Bible is to be interpreted theologically, and it is this kind of reading I will address in the subsequent chapters.

4

The Need for *Contextual* Theological Interpretation

What Is Theological Interpretation?

Theological interpretation is "interpretation of the Bible for the church."[1] More precisely, "Theological interpretation emphasizes the potentially mutual influence of Scripture and doctrine in theological discourse and, then, the role of Scripture in the self-understanding of the church and in critical reflection on the church's practices."[2] Theological interpretation of Scripture (TIS) has a starting point that

An earlier version of a portion of this chapter was previously published as "The Task of Reading the Bible for a Culturally Diverse North American Church" by Bo H. Lim, taken from *The Scripture and Hermeneutics Seminar: Retrospect and Prospect*, edited by Craig G. Bartholomew, David J. H. Beldman, Amber Bowen, and William Olhausen. Copyright © 2022 by Kirby Laing Centre for Public Theology in Cambridge. Used by permission of HarperCollins Christian Publishing. www.harpercollinschristian.com. An earlier version of another portion of this chapter was previously published as "Critical Methods and Critiques: Theological Interpretation" by Bo H. Lim, taken from *T&T Clark Handbook to Asian American Biblical Hermeneutics*, edited by Uriah Y. Kim and Seung Ai Yang. Copyright © 2019 by T&T Clark, an imprint of Bloomsbury Publishing Plc.

1. Bartholomew and Thomas, *Manifesto for Theological Interpretation*, ix.
2. J. Green, *Practicing Theological Interpretation*, 4.

is, as John Webster describes, "a dogmatic move: the reintegration of the authority of Scripture into the doctrine of God, which will have the effect of decisively redrawing the character of the church's affirmation of Scripture's authority."[3] In addition, TIS involves an ecclesial move by locating the interpretation of the Bible within the church's practices and tradition. This much all practitioners of TIS can agree on, but beyond this significant variation exists.

The discipline finds its origins among biblical scholars and theologians in the 1970s, with Karl Barth's theological commentary on Romans serving as its forerunner. Brevard Childs's canonical approach that claims the final form of the text is authoritative for the church began a new form of theological commentary writing.[4] Theologians considered "postcritical" or "postliberal," who also privileged the internal narrative structure of the Bible and the faith community's theological interests over historical reconstructions of the text, contributed to this discipline as well.[5] A similar return to interpreting sacred texts within one's faith tradition (as opposed to a so-called objective historical-critical method) occurred among Jewish scholars.[6] Daniel Treier identifies three markers of TIS:

1. Recovering the past: imitating precritical interpretation;
2. Reading within the rule(s): interacting with Christian doctrine; and
3. Reading with others: listening to the community of the Spirit.[7]

Given this description, it is not surprising that, with a few exceptions, TIS as a discipline primarily consists of conservative Protestant, Roman Catholic, and Eastern Orthodox theologians and biblical scholars.[8] Some scholars within this discipline have argued for the

---

3. Webster, *Holy Scripture*, 54.
4. See Childs, *Book of Exodus*; Childs, *Old Testament as Scripture*.
5. Kelsey, *Uses of Scripture*; Frei, *Eclipse of Biblical Narrative*; Lindbeck, *The Nature of Doctrine*; Fowl and Jones, *Reading in Communion*.
6. See Levenson, *Hebrew Bible*; Ochs, *Return to Scripture*.
7. Treier, *Introducing Theological Interpretation*, 20–33.
8. See, e.g., the list of contributors to the Brazos Theological Commentary on the Bible series. The exception would be the Belief series published by Westminster John Knox; see note 15 below.

"superiority of pre-critical exegesis"[9] because of its recognition of the multiple senses of Scripture, its focus on christological readings, and its formative role for the spiritual life.

TIS observes that the appeal of the ante-Nicene fathers, particularly Irenaeus and Tertullian, to the rule of faith as a summary of apostolic teaching served as a hermeneutical norm for the interpretation of Scripture, and that such a rule, or a nascent version of it, was operative in the formation of the canon. Since the rule is a summary of scriptural teaching contained in the Nicene and Apostles' creeds, individual texts are assumed to support, rather than contradict, trinitarian doctrine.[10] Some proponents of TIS advocate that Scripture reading is a communal spiritual practice and, therefore, methodological concerns are secondary to the moral commitments of the community of faith. For example, Stephen Fowl argues that "texts don't have ideologies,"[11] and therefore Christians ought to engage in underdetermined interpretation where "biblical interpretation will be the occasion of a complex interaction between the biblical text, and the varieties of theological, moral, material, political, and ecclesial concerns that are part of the day-to-day lives of Christians struggling to live faithfully before God in the contexts in which they find themselves."[12] Viewed in this manner, the hermeneutical task is not to determine a proper method of biblical study but rather to cultivate the moral virtues of truth seeking/telling, repentance, forgiveness, reconciliation, and patience necessary for the Holy Spirit to mediate the transformative power of the Scriptures in the church.

TIS scholarship has largely been a posthistorical, critical engagement of the Bible in and for white, theologically conservative Christian

---

9. Steinmetz, "Superiority of Pre-Critical Exegesis." As theological commentaries have proliferated, so too have commentaries on precritical interpretation, the translation and publication of patristic works, and studies on the reception history of the Bible.

10. Greene-McCreight, "Rule of Faith." Greene-McCreight observes that for Protestants, the rule of faith morphed away from creedal norms into *sui ipsius interpres*, the assumption that Scripture interprets itself and that it is noncontradictory.

11. Fowl, *Engaging Scripture*, 63–65.

12. Fowl, *Engaging Scripture*, 60. See Briggs, *Virtuous Reader*, for an examination of virtue ethics and reading the Old Testament.

contexts.[13] Historical criticism continues to be TIS's main interlocutor, with modern philosophy a distant second. Ideological criticism is seldom engaged.[14] With a few notable exceptions,[15] theological interpreters do not view contextual readings as theological, and contextual interpreters do not see their contexts acknowledged or valued by theological interpreters.[16] Little interaction occurs between TIS scholars and the authors of global or culture-specific Bible commentaries. One wonders what TIS as a discipline would look like if its practitioners engaged diverse social cultural contexts with the same dedication and rigor they engage other "nontheological" disciplines such as historical criticism and Western philosophy. The discipline is primarily populated by English-speaking scholars from the United Kingdom, Australia, New Zealand, Canada, and the United States. These scholars have sought to decenter Scripture study from historic concerns to

13. See the list of contributors and the range of topics covered in Bartholomew and Thomas, *Manifesto for Theological Interpretation*, and Goheen, *Reading the Bible Missionally*. In his essay in *Manifesto for Theological Interpretation*, Angus Paddison states, "Contextual interpretation *is* theological interpretation." "History and Reemergence," 38 (emphasis original). Yet neither he nor any of the authors in the volume engage contextual theology in any substantive manner.

14. Exceptions would be engagement with feminist criticism in Watson's *Text, Church and World*; Moberly's "Genesis 22" in his *Bible, Theology, and Faith*; and Lim and Castelo, *Hosea*. Treier concludes his *Introducing Theological Interpretation of Scripture* with a chapter titled "From the 'Western' Academy to the Global Church: Engaging Social Locations?" While Treier's acknowledgment of the importance of social contexts is encouraging, the chapter fails to acknowledge the ethnic diversity within Western Christianity and provides few guidelines for integrating social contexts into the process of TIS.

15. See the Westminster John Knox series Belief: A Theological Commentary on the Bible. As with other theological commentary series, the authors are theologians who seek to interpret the Bible for the church and who employ ecclesial resources. This series differs from others in that "the group of authors assembled for this series represents more diversity of race, ethnicity, and gender than any other commentary series. They approach the larger Christian tradition with a critical respect, seeking to reclaim its riches and at the same time to acknowledge its shortcomings." Placher and Pauw, introduction to *Mark*, xii–xiii. In addition, the contributors to the one volume *Theological Bible Commentary* recognize "acute attention to historical and social issues, concern for gender, ethnicity, and other dimensions of social location, concern for the formation of biblical literature and its traditions: all can yield theological insights." O'Day and Petersen, *Theological Bible Commentary*, viii.

16. A good example of this exclusion is the absence of Gutiérrez's *On Job* in any discussion of theological interpretation, even though this work meets the stated criteria of TIS.

theological foci and employ the resources of Christian and Jewish religious traditions rather than solely the tools of historical criticism. Many in the academy have not welcomed TIS for a variety of reasons. For some, TIS poses a threat to biblical studies' claim to be nonsectarian within the academy. Some worry that calling attention to the Bible's religious claims might lead people to question the Bible's privileged cultural status, and others fret that its religious focus will jeopardize what they deemed to be the objective results of biblical scholarship. Some accuse TIS of trying to insulate the Bible from critique, whether in the form of historical or ideological criticism, and to privilege certain religious groups as interpreters of the Bible. Some suspect TIS is a Trojan horse, conservative dogma masquerading as a legitimate academic discipline.

Practitioners of TIS claim that theological interpretation is an attempt to retrieve biblical interpretation for the sake of the church. Implied in such a statement is the belief that the historical interests of Bible scholars have too long dominated the agenda of biblical interpretation in the academy. Theologians have welcomed the opportunity to engage in biblical interpretation, as demonstrated by the proliferation of theological commentaries, and religious biblical scholars have enjoyed the freedom to be overt about their faith assumptions. It seems the jury is still out on whether clergy and congregations will benefit more from the contributions of TIS than from traditional forms of biblical scholarship.

No one scholar, school, or publication represents the breadth of TIS, but a sense of its hermeneutical concerns can be found in the eight-volume Scripture and Hermeneutics Series (Zondervan, 2000–2007). Six volumes in this series are devoted to methodology, and two are constructive works, one on reading the Gospel of Luke and the other on engaging the political theology of Oliver O'Donovan. The first volume, *Renewing Biblical Interpretation*, provides the framework for the volumes that follow. In its introduction, Craig Bartholomew identifies historical, literary, and theological issues as the three key elements necessary for a theologically informed model of biblical hermeneutics. He argues that biblical interpretation is shaped by philosophy, so the philosophy of history, literature, and theology must be engaged to define and determine a theological hermeneutic for Scripture.[17] Of the ten essays in this initial volume, four concern history, four address literature, and two focus on theology. While the remaining volumes in the series are not neatly divided into the categories of history, literature, and theology, the series' topics and titles indicate that these elements shape the series:

Vol. 1	Renewing Biblical Interpretation
Vol. 2	After Pentecost: Language and Biblical Interpretation
Vol. 3	A Royal Priesthood?: The Use of the Bible Ethically and Politically: A Dialogue with Oliver O'Donovan
Vol. 4	"Behind" the Text: History and Biblical Interpretation
Vol. 5	Out of Egypt: Biblical Theology and Biblical Interpretation
Vol. 6	Reading Luke: Interpretation, Reflection, Formation
Vol. 7	Canon and Biblical Interpretation
Vol. 8	The Bible and the University

While a focus on theology seems indispensable to TIS, I would question whether theological hermeneutics should continue to be primarily focused on the topics of theology, history, and literature. While TIS has moved away from philosophical discussions and focused more on doctrine and the church's tradition, Darren Sarisky's 2019 work, *Reading the Bible Theologically*, demonstrates that history and literature are still its primary foci.

History as an Evasion of Ideology

In *The Invention of the Biblical Scholar*, Stephen Moore and Yvonne Sherwood narrate the history of the scholarly study of the Bible. They acknowledge that until the early modern period, the Bible was read theologically in precisely the manner TIS scholars have championed. Moore and Sherwood write, "The essential and enabling rule for biblical scholarship from the second-century apologists down to the sixteenth-century Reformers was the rule of faith; it was that rule—actually a complex congeries of minute regulations and encompassing assumptions—that determined the enterprise of biblical

17. Bartholomew, introduction to *Renewing Biblical Interpretation*, xxvii.

scholarship down to its details."[18] Since the Enlightenment, history, or more precisely historical criticism, has dominated biblical study.

Moore and Sherwood bring to light a neglected aspect of this history, the early stages of the Enlightenment. By doing so they reframe how biblical studies' obsession with history ought to be viewed. They observe that early in the Enlightenment, what they consider the "first wave" of Enlightenment challenge to the Bible, the primary objections to the Bible were not historical but moral: "Early modern Europeans, engaging with the Bible as a social, political, and theological force and cultural exemplar, were concerned, above all, with questions of what Kant termed moral faith and conversely, *moral unbelief*."[19] Biblical "error" was not primarily historical, textual, or scientific, but rather of a moral nature. Moore and Sherwood write, "This debate on biblical error orbited obsessively around such iconic biblical crimes as the divinely mandated genocide of the Canaanites, Abraham's willingness to offer Isaac as a bloody sacrifice, and the manifest moral sins of David, the 'man after [God's] own heart' (Acts 13:22)."[20] They add, "Indeed, the early modern moral critique of the Bible, obsessed as it was with genocide, human sacrifice, and atonement theology, was concerned above all with crimes of blood."[21] One could think Moore and Sherwood are describing twenty-first-century challenges to the Bible made by postcolonial critics, not seventeenth-century objections made by Enlightenment thinkers. After four hundred years the exact same criticisms of the Bible have resurfaced, and history is repeating itself.

What happened next reveals much about the nature of the discipline and poses a contemporary challenge to contemporary biblical scholars and theologians facing similar issues. Moore and Sherwood narrate a step-by-step succession of events in what they call the "second wave" of the Enlightenment:

1. Because biblical scholars were incapable of responding adequately to the moral challenges posed to the Bible, they turned

---

18. Moore and Sherwood, *Invention*, 47.
19. Moore and Sherwood, *Invention*, 49 (emphasis original).
20. Moore and Sherwood, *Invention*, 50.
21. Moore and Sherwood, *Invention*, 54.

to focus solely on historical concerns. Moore and Sherwood write, "After the eighteenth century, the investigation of biblical morality was quietly dropped from the job description of the biblical scholar. This was because the moral questions put to the Bible by the early rationalists were deemed to be irresolvable and socially corrosive, whereas historical questions were (or so it was imagined) resolvable and less incendiary."[22]

2. The focus on history allowed the Bible to be exempted from theological and ethical debates. In this environment, biblical scholarship could continue to thrive and avoid becoming entangled within the culture wars of its day.

3. By avoiding theology, biblical scholars were able to legitimate their academic standing and cultural respectability while maintaining their theological and ecclesial commitments, since theology and history no longer overlapped. Moore and Sherwood write, "The removal of the theological as the target of critical inquiry ensured that he [the biblical scholar] could be both a skeptic and a believer at one and the same time. It became possible to be at once Christian and 'modern,' theologically orthodox yet simultaneously skeptical of the Bible's historicity—though a complex series of markers were set in place to regulate how far one might push one's skepticism."[23]

4. Once established within the academy, the Bible became part of the canon within the humanities curriculum. Moore and Sherwood observe, "Responding to the loss of theological authority, the Bible was rehabilitated on human and cultural grounds in the eighteenth century. The Bible was re-universalized, so to speak, and its relevance newly perpetuated in such unlikely domains as philology, ancient history, archaeology, ancient Near Eastern languages, and the quest for the ever-elusive authorial hand."[24]

Moore and Sherwood demonstrate that biblical scholars could not adequately address the theological and ethical objections to the

---

22. Moore and Sherwood, *Invention*, 59–60.
23. Moore and Sherwood, *Invention*, 61.
24. Moore and Sherwood, *Invention*, x.

Bible, so they pivoted to focus on historical concerns to avoid their critics. By doing so, scholars could eschew thorny theological issues and focus on safer, less controversial topics. Biblical scholars would go on to establish themselves as reputable academics and avoid ideological concerns since the latter were too contentious. By reinventing the sacred text of the Bible into a cultural icon, they were able to neutralize ethical objections and maintain academic credibility. However, as I demonstrate in chapter 3, in the past several decades critical studies have taken aim at both the religious and cultural hegemonic influences of the Bible. The moral and ethical objections to the study of the Bible are aimed even at those who do not consider it sacred. Biblical scholarship as an academic discipline survived the intellectual critique of the Enlightenment, but it remains to be seen whether it will survive the ethical critique of postcolonial thinkers.

The same motivations for fixating on textual and historical matters continue to be true today in biblical studies. Reputable universities confer doctoral degrees in biblical studies to both the atheist and the fundamentalist without ever challenging their religious beliefs since their work remains technical and ideological commitments make no difference. In an academy that rewards specialization, biblical scholars can focus on textual or historical minutiae to avoid ideological or theological controversies. One wonders whether the fixation on history and literature by scholars continues a strategy to avoid the more difficult ideological and ethical questions posed to the Bible. It is strikes me that the last volume in the Scripture and Hermeneutics Series, *The Bible and the University*, continues to focus on history and literature and neglects to address ideological challenges to the Bible. It was published in 2007, well after universities were rife with issues of race, gender, colonialism, and more. It seems that either the editors and authors did not think these issues were important to the church and academy, or they evaded them and focused instead on safer topics like history and literature.

This omission may be the result of the lack of cultural diversity among the series' scholars. As I argue earlier in this book, the most dramatic shifts in biblical hermeneutics take place due to changes in the Bible's readership. While some white male theologians may consider engagement with critical studies and contextual theologies

marginal to their personal and professional lives, many women and
theologians of color see these issues as front and center for their
identities and vocations, particularly when they live and work in
predominantly white contexts. For example, Robert Romero begins
his book *Brown Church* by telling the story of Rosa, a Latina Christian, who goes off to a prestigious university where she experiences
a religious crisis not because she hears the challenge "God is dead!,"
but rather she hears, "Christianity is a white man's religion" and
"Christianity is the colonizer's religion."[25] In the twenty-first century
virtually every Christian of color and female Christian will have to
address the accusations of colonialism and patriarchy. Theologians
of color and female theologians find it necessary to engage critical
studies and contextual theologies because of the church's entangle-
ments with slavery, racism, sexism, and the oppression of Indigenous
populations. These inquiries are not only intellectual pursuits but
also existential and pastoral concerns since they directly relate to
one's own sense of Christian and cultural identity and the integrity
of the church's witness.

Since these matters are often personal, scholars of color and
female scholars are often required to transgress conventional academic boundaries by including themselves or their communities as
subjects of inquiry.[26] Doing so requires vulnerability and personal
and professional risk but nevertheless is done out of a love for one's
underrepresented community and a desire to serve the global church.
Autobiography as theology is not a new genre, but when scholars
from underrepresented groups engage it they subject themselves
and their communities to what Toni Morrison has referred to as the
"white gaze."[27] Kwame Bediako, whose published dissertation is titled
Theology and Identity, speaks from his own experience: "The issue
of identity in turn forced the theologian to become the locus of his
struggle for integration through a dialogue which, to be authentic,
was bound to become personal and so infinitely more intense. The
African Christian theologian is quite often 'handling dynamite, his

25. Romero, *Brown Church*, 1–2.
26. Choy's *Ancestral Feeling* is but one example of where personal and professional boundaries are transgressed for the sake of academic argument.
27. Greenfield-Sanders, *Toni Morrison: The Pieces I Am*, 6:31.

own past, his people's present,' a far cry from 'the clinical observations of the sort one might make about Babylonian religion.'"[28]

The work of underrepresented scholars, when deeply personal, will not only be subjected to the criticism of the academy but will also be scrutinized by their own communities to see whether they have betrayed their own culture and faith. Contextual theology involves holding two sticks of dynamite simultaneously, and the mishandling of either can result in the accusation of being an "Uncle Tom" or a heretic. In Bediako's case, his quest for an African Christian theology required him to define the fundamental nature of Christianity as well as what it meant to be truly African.[29] As evidenced in Bediako's own testimony, conversion for many Christians of color involves both the relinquishment and redemption of cultural identity.

If theological interpretation is to equip ministers of the gospel, then its hermeneutical and theological foci must broaden. If the church is *semper reformanda* and biblical-theological interpretation is to serve the church, then biblical and theological studies too must be *semper reformanda*. I am in no way suggesting that TIS scholarship be displaced by contextual interpretation. Rather, I am arguing for more reflexive discourse between the two so that they might mutually benefit and be transformed through the interchange.

The hermeneutical foci must change to include ideological, cultural, and moral issues in biblical interpretation. While biblical scholars may object that my proposal redefines the traditional understanding of the discipline, Moore and Sherwood have demonstrated that its present focus on history and literature is the aberration. The discipline of theological interpretation claims to retrieve ecclesial interpretation by reading the Bible christocentrically, figurally, and sacramentally to form Christian disciples, but this is a selective reappropriation of the tradition. Neglected in this retrieval of the church's tradition is the attention given by past interpreters to apologetic issues. Many of the church's critics raised historical or textual difficulties, but much of the criticism leveled against the Bible concerned moral and ethical

28. Bediako, *Jesus and the Gospel*, 53; here he quotes from Walls, *Missionary Movement*, 13.
29. Sara Fretheim does the important work of understanding Bediako and his impact within the African intellectual tradition in *Kwame Bediako*.

matters. If TIS is to reclaim ecclesial interpretation, then it must return to the church's historic task of addressing moral and ideological challenges to the Christian faith rather than focusing solely on historical, literary, and philosophical objections.[30]

Theological Interpretation Is Not Sufficiently Theological

Is the Christian tradition sufficiently capable of policing its own? That is, should the church adopt "nontheological" resources into its theological and ministerial methods? While it certainly may be aspirational, Fowl's assertion that "the ecclesial contexts in which theological interpretation of Scripture finds its proper home also provides adequate means of dealing with sinful and failed interpretation apart from a rigorous hermeneutical method"[31] is unfortunately too optimistic. A case in point is John Wesley, who in his 1757 work *The Doctrine of Sin According to Scripture, Reason, and Experience* presented Africans as the worst manifestation of sin in the world, only to make a complete turnaround on the topic in his 1774 work *Thoughts upon Slavery*.[32] This reversal occurred not through the study of Scripture or theology but rather through receiving better and more accurate information from the field of "African studies" of his day. In his 1774 argument against slavery, Wesley used historical criticism to reject the claims of early British travelers and socioanthropologists to refute the arguments for African inferiority. Sègbégnon Gnonhossou notes that "a geopolitical conversion"[33] was necessary to change British minds on the topic of slavery, as was the case for Wesley, whose own transformation relied on nontheological and nonecclesial resources. J. Kameron Carter asks why it took fifteen centuries between fourth-century Gregory of Nyssa and nineteenth-century abolitionists for the church to take a univocal stand against slavery. He writes, "This presents a disturbing situation for those who advocate reading the Scriptures theologically, a situation that

---

30. John Thompson's *Reading the Bible with the Dead* is one of the few works on the history of reception that engages contemporary ideological criticism.
31. Fowl, *Theological Interpretation of Scripture*, 53.
32. Wesley, *Doctrine of Original Sin*; Wesley, *Thoughts upon Slavery*.
33. Gnonhossou, "Who Were the Enslaved?," 7.

can no longer be evaded; namely, that one can read Scripture within the theological grammar of the Christian faith and yet do so in such a way as to read within and indeed theologically sanction, if not sanctify, as Michel Foucault says, 'the order of things.'"[34]

Willie Jennings observes that Western Christianity has suffered from a diseased social imagination where it is unable to think theologically about identity because of its patterns of colonial dominance. Jennings takes aim at the kind of virtue ethics, intellectual holism, and rational and moral formation proposed by Alasdair MacIntyre, whose work is influential to many proponents of TIS.[35] He narrates the tale of José de Acosta, who embodied the best of the Christian theological tradition yet nevertheless operated within the colonialist logic of the conquistadors. The result was that the "inner coherence of traditioned Christian inquiry was grafted onto the inner coherence of colonialism,"[36] and this "new trajectory established a strange kind of insularity and circularity for Christian traditions of inquiry."[37] This tradition went on to employ biblical literacy as a tool for promulgating a national consciousness. Judgments on who was capable and incapable of articulating orthodoxy were racialized from the outset, and determinations were made about which literary works possessed a theological aesthetic and which did not. Jennings argues that the Western Christian theological tradition is diseased with the ideology of white supremacy and an imperialist matrix that has been disseminated though its vast network of relationships. If contemporary Christians naively appropriate the resources of the church's tradition and ignore its history of oppression, they are prone to repeating the same mistakes. Jennings concludes, "Thus, the question for living Israel and the church is not, how do we form faithful people, but what does it mean to form faithful people, given the complex social situations for our theological pedagogies?"[38]

Theological interpretation operates on the assumption that "the text we call the Bible was put together in the first place by the same

34. Carter, *Race*, 233.
35. See MacIntyre, *After Virtue*; MacIntyre, *Whose Justice?*
36. Jennings, *Christian Imagination*, 83.
37. Jennings, *Christian Imagination*, 83.
38. Jennings, *Christian Imagination*, 285.

community that now needs to interpret it."[39] By recovering early church beliefs and practices, proponents of TIS consider themselves the rightful heirs qualified to interpret the Bible. The inherent danger is that this approach too closely identifies the modern church with Israel and the apostles and runs the risk of claiming scriptural warrant for its own hegemonic practices. Critics of TIS such as Carter and Jennings stress the differences between the modern church and the Bible's ancient authors. In the story of Jesus's encounter with the Canaanite woman in Matthew 15:21–28, Jennings identifies the modern church not with Israel but with the *goyim*.[40] He believes a healthy distancing between Israel and the contemporary church is important to properly read the Scriptures theologically. All Christians benefit from contextual readings even when they are not directed toward their culture or communities since by their "foreignness" they remind all non-Jewish Christians of their gentile status. In fact, it is not uncommon for contextual interpreters to focus on the "foreigner" in biblical texts, and one might argue the most thorough interpretation on such topics have been done by contextual interpreters.[41] The current practice of TIS neglects the varied social and cultural contexts of the contemporary church and the historical legacy of the church in these communities. All Christians are located at a significant cultural and historical distance from the ancient Scriptures, all Christians read the text contextually, and all Christians need to engage the Bible critically, lest they be held captive to their culture's idols.

TIS is a conscious effort by those in ecclesial communities to read the Bible with the resources found within the church, such as its own

39. Jenson, "Religious Power of Scripture," 98.
40. Jennings, *Christian Imagination*, 262. Mark Brett observes that the relationship between Jews and gentiles in the Old Testament is repeatedly contested, so Jennings's reading does not account for the diversity within the biblical witnesses. *Political Trauma and Healing*, 9. See Brett's *Decolonizing God* for a treatment of this diversity.
41. In Asian American contextual interpretation alone, see Hertig and Sun, *Mirrored Reflections*; C. Kim, "Reading the Cornelius Story"; G. Kim, *Embracing the Other*; J. Kim, "Empowerment or Enslavement?"; U. Kim, "Uriah the Hittite"; Kwok, "Finding Ruth a Home"; Lee, "Ruth the Moabite"; T. Lim, "Ruth's Hebrew"; Moy, "Resident Aliens"; Ngan, "Neither Here nor There"; Pa, "Reading Ruth 3:1–5"; Rietz, "Identifying with the Exodus"; Yamada, "Manzanar"; Yee, "She Stood in Tears."

interpretive traditions and spiritual practices. Yet the church's tradition and theological resources have often neglected the contributions of missiology. Lamin Sanneh argues that a fundamental characteristic of the Christian faith is its ability to be translated into different languages and cultures.[42] Early on, linguistic and cultural translation was a key theological resource of and necessity for the church that was neglected later in the age of Christendom. The rise of globalization has required the church to resurrect this ancient ministry practice in domestic contexts. While the message of the Scriptures has often been constrained by the cultural ideologies of its messengers, the Bible has also had a transformative impact on communities exposed to its teachings.[43]

Yet since translation requires missionaries to learn new languages and cultures, more than translation was always needed, and ideally a mutual exchange of ideas was to take place. In order to do this with theological integrity, a renewed doctrine of creation was necessary. Jennings writes, "To enter a new land was to enter a newness that required careful listening to the rhythms of creation played by the indigenous peoples so that the sounds of Christian witness might be joined in harmony (with its proper dissonance) with those rhythms. Moreover, to enter a new land was to touch the skin of a people, joining skin to skin, with the inevitability of being changed, or being transformed, not simply by the people but by creation itself."[44]

Mark Brett argues that "the church needs to develop not just a more adequate postcolonial theology, but in addition, to develop a repertoire of postcolonial practices."[45] The most prominent among these practices is "self-emptying" (or *kenosis*) and a relinquishment of political control. Unfortunately, the mutual exchange of ideas that Jennings writes about often did not occur; instead, the relationships were one-sided and exploitative. The disciple of Jesus in the

---

42. Sanneh, *Translating the Message*.

43. See, e.g., Marsh, *Beloved Community*.

44. Jennings, *Christian Imagination*, 114. Jennings goes on to narrate the tragic tale of the nineteenth-century Bishop Colenso. He sought to translate the gospel to the Zulu culture, but because he lacked the theological sophistication for genuine cultural engagement, he unwittingly imposed English nationalism in the guise of Christian theology.

45. Brett, *Political Trauma and Healing*, 5.

twenty-first century does not join a group of peasants following an itinerant preacher in the Galilean countryside but rather the largest religion the world has ever known that was exported through empires. Christians today inevitably have to address the church's past colonial sins so as not to repeat them in the present. If TIS is not a method but a moral, communal, and spiritual practice, its communities must be marked by humility, openness, and mutual and transformative exchange with new cultures in order to be effective. If contextual interpretation is to be received and valued by the church, its people will need to be open to the possibility of a new kind of church. In the face of rapid globalization and increasing nativism, the fear of diversity and change may motivate a disinterest in contextual interpretation by some sectors of the church, who instead choose insularity within their own traditions. Yet Andrew Walls offers the reminder that "the faith of Christ is infinitely translatable, it creates 'a place to feel at home.' *But it must not make a place where we are so much at home that no one else can live there.* Here we have no abiding city."[46] The church is made up of pilgrim people who are constantly on the move so "home" is never a fixed reality.

TIS defines itself as "biblical interpretation oriented to the knowledge of God."[47] Given the influential reach and high stakes of "pastoral power,"[48] the question of in what way biblical interpretations qualify as God-talk must be interrogated. *The Art of Reading Scripture* lists "Nine Theses of the Interpretation of Scripture," and one thesis is that "Christians need to read the Bible in dialogue with diverse others outside the church."[49] Yet the only "diverse others" any of the authors engage are Jewish interpreters. The authors of the *Manifesto for Theological Interpretation* assert that "Theological Interpretation [is] for All of Life" and write, "To move in this direction, as we must, the comprehensive scope of Scripture will need to be recovered, the time in our culture(s) discerned, and the hard

---

46. Walls, *Missionary Movement*, 25 (emphasis added).

47. Vanhoozer, "What Is Theological Interpretation?," 24.

48. Foucault describes this form of power as that exercised by clergy through a network of relations that carries influence over individual, communities, and even the state. "Subject and Power," as cited in Jennings, *Christian Imagination*, 107–8.

49. Davis and Hays, *Art of Reading Scripture*, 4–5.

work done of moving back and forth between these two poles, so that Scripture is heard in relation to all of life."[50] Astonishingly and disconcertingly, the authors claim that few scholars today successfully engage in this work, despite the recent surge of publications in this field. Several notable proponents of TIS quote the words of Johann Bengel to define its task: "*Te totum applica ad textum, rem totam applica ad te*—'Apply your whole self to the text; apply the whole subject matter to yourself.'"[51] When interpreting the Scriptures theologically Moberly confesses, "All the contexts that I inhabit and that form my identity—church and university, neighborhood and country, home and work—should in some way (albeit variously) be recognized to bear upon the task."[52] If this is the case, the current practitioners of TIS fail to execute what they conceive of as the task of TIS. They may have succeeded in the goal of recovering the comprehensive scope of the Bible, and they may have thoroughly engaged the disciplines of history and philosophy. But few have successfully discerned the relationship between Scripture and contemporary culture so as to apply Scripture to all of life. If they have successfully done so, they have still neglected the concerns and needs of significance populations within the church.

My criticism that TIS is not sufficiently contextual is based on its own stated criteria. Those engaged in theological interpretation and biblical scholarship from trinitarian and evangelical perspectives have increasingly acknowledged the importance of diverse readings of Scripture. They have extensively written on the methodology of biblical and theological interpretation regarding historical, literary, and theological matters, but very little has been done on the topic of cultural diversity. Darren Sarisky, in his recent work on theological interpretation, observes that the lacuna in TIS scholarship is theological reflection on reading and readers. He writes, "The hermeneutic proposed here assumed that it is neither actually possible nor genuinely desirable for readers 'to strip off all our particularities— particularities of gender, race, nationality, religion, social class,

---

50. Bartholomew and Thomas, *Manifesto for Theological Interpretation*, 25.
51. Moberly, "What Is Theological Interpretation?," 168. See also Hays, "Reading the Bible," 15.
52. Moberly, "What Is Theological Interpretation?," 168.

age—and enter [upon proper inquiry] purely as normal adult human beings.'"[53] So while in theory diverse contextual interpretation is the domain of TIS, their practice has not lived up to their claims.

I am committed to the theological interpretation of Scripture because TIS, at least in theory, values the biblical interpretation of the church in the Global South and East and multicultural evangelical communities in Europe and North America. Ironically, it is academic "contextual interpreters" who disregard these contributions, as do conservative Christians who worry of heterodoxy. In the remainder of this work, I will explore what a methodology for reading the Bible theologically in diverse cultural contexts might look like.

53. Sarisky, *Reading the Bible Theologically*, 188–89, quoting Wolterstorff, "Travail of Theology," 38.

Part Two

AN INTEGRATED MODEL OF BIBLICAL INTERPRETATION

5

Contextual and Theological Interpretation in the Global Church

∘❀∘

Postcolonial Christian Interpretation

Richard Hays defines theological interpretation of Scripture (TIS) by saying it should "remain close to the primary language of the witnesses rather than moving away from the particularity of the biblical testimony to a language of second-order abstraction that seeks to 'translate' the biblical imagery into some other conceptual register."[1] This definition rules out much of contextual biblical interpretation and, I would add, much of theological interpretation. It disqualifies contextual theologies that have used Indigenous concepts in their hermeneutics. For example, Asian American theology and biblical interpretation have employed motifs of marginality, liminality, *tao*, *han*, *jeong*, and *yin* and *yang*, and Hays seems to believe such concepts ought to be rejected. Yet one need not delve deep into the church's doctrinal traditions before encountering "second-order abstractions" and non-biblical "conceptual registers" such as the Trinity. Western theology has a legacy of translating the biblical testimony into nonbiblical cultural concepts. Hays qualifies his definition when he

1. Hays, "Reading the Bible," 13–14.

writes, "We can never approach the Bible as though we were the first ones to read it—or the first to read it appropriately. . . . Consequently, *theological exegesis will find hermeneutical aid, not hindrance, in the church's doctrinal traditions.*"[2]

For Hays it appears that nonbiblical concepts approved by the church's tradition are acceptable, but others are not. He likely has in mind the adoption of nonbiblical concepts by the likes of Paul Tillich and Rudolf Bultmann and the failed project of twentieth-century Protestant liberal theology, but Hays's cultural myopia is quite obvious. His vision for theological interpretation does not take into consideration the missional vocation for the church. While his methods may guard against heterodoxy, they may also result in an orthodoxy that is culturally insular, ministerially ineffective, and potentially oppressive in multicultural contexts.

For example, Elizabeth Mburu argues that because African Christians have not sufficiently contextualized theology into their culture, they lead dichotomized lives.[3] For her, effective ministry of the gospel requires translation, and as Lamin Sanneh says, such theologizing has been part of the fabric of Christian ministry from its very inception.[4] It is much easier to reject nonbiblical concepts yet embrace the Christian tradition when the tradition arrives in culturally familiar forms and when one's people have not experienced the scourge of colonialism. In contrast to Hays, K. K. Yeo argues that theological interpretation *is* cross-cultural interpretation and that the sacredness of Scripture allows it to be translated across cultures. He goes on to employ a wide range of Chinese cultural and religious motifs in his engagement with the Bible.[5] Like the proponents of TIS, Yeo provides *theological* justification for his hermeneutics, in this case the Christian doctrines of loving one's neighbor and the eschatological vision of a multicultural church.

The question I explore in this chapter is, What counts as the church's doctrinal tradition? Almost all agree on the authority of patristic theologians, but beyond that the consensus dissolves. William

2. Hays, "Reading the Bible," 14–15 (emphasis original).
3. Mburu, *African Hermeneutics*, 6–8.
4. Sanneh, *Translating the Message*, 13–96.
5. Yeo, "Response: Multicultural Readings."

Abraham's *Canonical Theism* project draws the line of theological authority at the first millennium, but this move is undoubtedly quite arbitrary, though convenient. A quick perusal of the most influential theologians for TIS scholars reveals familiar names: Augustine, Aquinas, John Calvin, Martin Luther, John Wesley, and Karl Barth. Yet the "canon" is not closed, since even after Barth, TIS scholars have looked to Henri de Lubac, John Yoder, Robert Jenson, and John Webster.[6] So the church's doctrinal traditions that Hays speaks of are a living tradition; it is rooted in the patristic authors and the ecumenical creeds, but it is not limited to them.

The challenge that many people of color and women face with the church's tradition is that their communities may possess little connection to it in the present and may even have been historically marginalized by this same church. This is one reason female scholars and scholars of color view TIS with suspicion. Many liberation and postcolonial theologians propose that the only way forward is to adopt or create new traditions unencumbered by the church's colonial past.

I have already indicated that I write for a global Christian communion that affirms trinitarian and evangelical doctrines and therefore sees validity in the church's tradition, even if only implicitly. So how are they to engage it? John Mbiti observes "that 'mission Christianity' had produced a church 'trying to exist without a theology' and 'without theological consciousness and concern.'"[7] The church's doctrinal tradition certainly can be a helpful resource to address this problem. But if the only option to engage the tradition is from within the trappings of Western culture, doing so may unwittingly perpetuate colonial ideologies and practices. Not only should Christians of color reject solely appropriating the Western Christian tradition, but all Christians ought to do so. Here lies the contribution of theologians outside Europe and North America who have thought more deeply about colonialism because of their context. Their contribution is not only for the African or Chinese church; it also helps Western Christians better discern the relationship between theology and

---

6. East, *The Church's Book.*
7. Bediako, *Jesus and the Gospel*, 16. Bediako cites Mbiti, *African Religions and Philosophy*, 232, and Mbiti, "Some African Concepts," 51.

culture. Is a postcolonial reappropriation of the church's tradition possible and even desirable? I highlight two examples of non-Western theologians doing so in very different manners: Kwame Bediako and Renie Choy.

Bediako has been described as the greatest African theologian of his time, but he may very well be the greatest theologian of this current generation of world Christianity. His impact has long been felt within global Christianity, as evidenced in the fact that the annual conference of the International Fellowship for Mission as Transformation (INFEMIT) bears his name along with John Stott. His theological contributions will be increasingly appreciated within Europe and North America due to recent publications about him.[8] Tim Hartman summarizes Bediako's theology saying, "Christianity is indigenous to Africa. African Christians have their own distinct history rooted in patristic Christian theology and traditional African cultures and religions."[9] Like the practitioners of TIS, Bediako turns to patristic authors to ground his theology, and like both TIS and contextual interpreters, Bediako is critical of academic biblical studies and historical criticism. Hartman describes Bediako's view of biblical scholarship: "Specifically when considering biblical studies, 'the historical-critical method of exegesis, a legacy of Enlightenment methodology, which belongs to just a segment of Western intellectual history,' needs to be given up because it is a product of Western hegemony, not a model passed down from 'the Old Testament prophets, not our Lord Jesus, nor his apostles.'"[10] Where Bediako differs from TIS and agrees with postcolonial critics is that he sees in the Western theological tradition a syncretistic form of Western culture and therefore considers it inadequate to serve the people of Africa. Yet he

---

8. Hartman, *Theology After Colonization*; Hartman, *Kwame Bediako*. While this is to be celebrated, it is lamentable that one of the greatest theologians of our time requires mediation by a Western scholar to be appreciated in the West. Bediako was prolific, but the majority of his writing did not take the form of monographs. Rather, they were articles scattered throughout various publications. This form of situational writing demonstrates his commitment to address the most pressing theological challenges of his context. It is, in Marcella Althaus-Reid's terms, more "chaotic" and displays a commitment to grassroots Christianity.

9. Hartman, *Kwame Bediako*, 62.

10. Hartman, *Kwame Bediako*, 108.

departs from both the practitioners of TIS and postcolonial critics in his theological method by seeking to recover a precolonial version of Indigenous Christianity that is rooted in African primal religious traditions.

In Bediako we see a trinitarian, evangelical, contextual, and theological interpretation of Scripture that is ecclesial by its commitment to grassroots African Christianity. He affirms Mbiti who writes, "African Christianity cannot wait for written theology to keep pace with it. . . . Academic theology can only come afterwards and examine the features retrospectively in order to understand them."[11] Bediako's hermeneutic is theological in its commitment to the theology of the early church fathers, postcolonial (a term he eschews in favor of "precolonial") in its suspicion of the Western theological tradition, and contextual in finding its substructure in African religious traditions. He wholeheartedly believes that "the faith of Christ is infinitely translatable,"[12] and he justifies the theological significance of the vernacular by appealing to the patristic use of the Greek translation of the Old Testament, the Septuagint, as Holy Scripture.[13] In contrast to Western syncretism, Bediako believes that "it may be that in Africa the opportunity lost in Europe for a serious and creative theological encounter between the Christian and primal traditions, can be regained."[14] African Christian theology done in this manner serves Africans and offers a model for all Christians to discern syncretistic elements of their faith and how they might more faithfully and effectively engage in ministry for their cultural contexts.

Much can be said about Bediako's theology, but for the purposes of this book, I will focus on his published dissertation, *Theology and Identity: The Impact of Culture upon Christian Thought in the Second Century and in Modern Africa*. Bediako demonstrates that the early church fathers had the same theological task as African theologians in the late twentieth century. Just as the early fathers sought "to establish an authentic Christian identity within their [Greco-Roman] culture, meaningful both for them and for the world as it was then

11. Mbiti, *Bible and Theology*, 229, as quoted in Bediako, *Jesus and the Gospel*, 17.
12. Walls, *Missionary Movement*, 25.
13. See chap. 6 for further discussion.
14. Bediako, *Jesus and the Gospel*, 59.

known,"[15] African theologians sought to do the same within their culture of African religious traditions. In the first half of the book, Bediako examines how Tatian, Tertullian, Justin, and Clement each addressed the relationship between the gospel and their Greco-Roman culture. Each differed in their conclusions, but they all recognized "the problem of identity for Christians of Graeco-Roman culture was that sooner or later the convert had to settle accounts with his past and his own cultural tradition."[16] Tertullian largely rejected the Greco-Roman tradition, Tatian argued for the historical priority of the Jewish-Christian tradition, and Justin and Clement tried to take the best of it for the sake of the gospel. By examining these early church fathers, Bediako establishes his methods and findings firmly within the orthodox, ecumenical, and precolonial Christian tradition.

In the book's second half, Bediako analyzes the work of four African theologians: Bolajo Idowu, John Mbiti, Mulago gwa Cikala Musharhamina, and Byang Kato. Just as the early church fathers were compelled to give an account of Greco-Roman culture for the sake of Christian witness, "no self-respecting theological institution in Africa can now avoid the study of African Traditional Religions."[17] These African theologians, like the church fathers, had varying views on the relationship between Christ and culture, so while Bediako is most sympathetic to Mbiti, he acknowledges a range of legitimate options. His central thesis is that the fathers and his African contemporaries were engaged in the same theological task to discern cultural identity. By examining culture, a notoriously elusive yet immensely important topic, the theological task has a scope and aim that is no less than a *théologie totale*.[18] In *Jesus and the Gospel in Africa*, Bediako recalls how a Western missionary preached the gospel in West Africa for nine years and converted fifty-two people, and how an African evangelist preached for two years and converted 120,000 persons. Whereas the Western missionary failed to present a *théologie totale*, the African evangelist, known as Prophet Harris, assumed the African spiritual universe, what Bediako refers to as the primal imagination. Bediako

15. Bediako, *Theology and Identity*, 33.
16. Bediako, *Theology and Identity*, 32.
17. Bediako, *Theology and Identity*, 434.
18. See my comments on this concept in chap. 7.

writes, "Because primal world-views are fundamentally religious, the primal imagination restores to theology the crucial dimension of living religiously for which the theologian needs make no apology. The primal imagination may help us restore the ancient unity of theology and spirituality."[19] Understanding cultural identity is not merely an academic exercise or a personal quest, but it is an attempt to define authentic Christianity and effective ministry at the grassroots level. African theology's understanding of the primal imagination is instructive for Africans and for all Christians.

Bediako concludes *Theology and Identity* by reflecting on how African theology ought to be understood within the Christian tradition. He laments how African theology's theological reflection on its pre-Christian heritage is too often categorized solely in terms of social anthropology. Since he sees African theology as analogous to the patristic phase of Christianity, he believes it ought to be understood within Christian history and the Christian tradition. He concludes the book by citing John Mbiti's description of how culture both snatches people away from and drives people toward Christ.[20] He writes, "Perhaps nothing demonstrates more clearly that the theological achievement of early Hellenistic Christianity in the second century and the emergent theological self-consciousness of African Christianity in the twentieth century, *belong to one and the same story*."[21] Viewed in this manner, the African Christian tradition is the church's doctrinal tradition. Thus, Hays's claim that "*theological exegesis will find hermeneutical aid, not hindrance, in the church's doctrinal traditions*"[22] means Christian readers of Scripture can find a hermeneutical aid in Bediako as well as in Augustine. That is, the church's tradition continues to mature as the church continues to grow, expand, and diversify. Andrew Walls observes "how the crossing of cultural frontiers develops and enlarges theology,"[23] and Van Engen goes further to say, "Each step forward, each 'translation' of

19. Bediako, *Jesus and the Gospel*, 95.
20. Mbiti, "African Indigenous Culture," 94, as cited in Bediako, *Theology and Identity*, 441.
21. Bediako, *Theology and Identity*, 441 (emphasis added).
22. Hays, "Reading the Bible," 14–15 (emphasis original).
23. Walls, "Globalization," 74.

the gospel offers the possibility of discovering something about God revealed in the Bible that no one has previously seen."[24] Whereas some may view the current plurality of approaches to biblical studies as a return to Babel, others celebrate it as a sign of Pentecost.

Choy has a different approach from Bediako to engaging the Christian tradition from a postcolonial perspective. She too is trinitarian and committed to the ministry of the gospel, yet her heritage of faith is rooted in Chinese Baptist congregations and now British Anglicanism. Choy is a historian and observes that while theologians' new postcolonial paradigms may displace traditional methods, they do not address the historical dilemmas. When critiquing Sang Hyun Lee's proposal for an Asian American liminal theology, Choy writes, "God may very well be 'liminal,' but the historic Christianity that communicated him was anything but."[25] The historic dilemma is the same central quest in Bediako's theology—the understanding of one's cultural identity and their faith in the gospel. Choy's concern for history certainly reflects her academic interests, but it is also integral to her theology and spirituality. She says "that notions of ancestral bond cannot be circumvented, because the language of family, generations, forefathers, progenitors, inheritance and heritage permeate nearly every page of Scripture from the Old to the New, and Christians have never been able to think about faith as something other than 'received' and 'passed on.'"[26]

Choy is critical of how the expansion of world Christianity continues to be described in Eurocentric terms, yet she acknowledges that at a historical level a focus on Europe is inescapable, and "to understand global Christianity . . . one must always understand Western European Christianity first."[27] Historical works demonstrating how early Christianity took root in in the Middle East, Africa, and Asia do not address the fact that the current expansion of world Christianity is not historically rooted in these traditions but rather in the Western tradition. While contemporary theologians pay homage to the fact that the church's earliest fathers like Augustine were African,

24. Van Engen, "The Glocal Church," 175.
25. Choy, *Ancestral Feeling*, 57.
26. Choy, *Ancestral Feeling*, xv.
27. Choy, *Ancestral Feeling*, 12.

Choy highlights that their contributions have been mediated via the West. She demonstrates that "it is therefore naïve to think that simply recalling his North African birthplace will solve the problem of Western dominance in the history of Christianity."[28] Attempts to portray Christianity as a global faith simply by highlighting the African or Asian origins of some of its early leaders are nothing more than theological tokenism. She critiques Sanneh's claims that the translation of the Bible led to Indigenous, decolonized versions of the Christian faith,[29] saying they do not sufficiently acknowledge the fact that more than the Bible was translated into cultures. Failing to acknowledge this reality can be potentially harmful, and Choy cites the example of how the fifteen million southern African Christians who currently identify as "Zionist" can trace their beliefs back to a Scotsman based in Melbourne in the 1880s. She writes, "The major problem with speaking as though there can be one lineage for Western Christianity and a different one for African Christianity is that it does not recognize the 'elective affinities' global Christians possess in addition to the ethnic affinities."[30]

Here lies the historical and theological challenge: European Christianity is the heritage of world Christianity for the majority of Christians today. For all the anticolonial and anti-imperial criticisms made by Christians of color, Choy notes that "empire explains Christianity's racial diversity."[31] That is, their ancestors became Christians after Western missionaries introduced Christ to various cultures around the world. Therefore, it is impossible for the majority of Christians today to fully "decolonize" their theology and return to a precolonial version of the faith.

Yet Choy also observes that the historical spread of Christianity is much more complicated than postcolonial critics portray. She offers a corrective to a unidirectional linear approach to historicizing spiritual heritages by tracing the vast and varied influences that led to her own conversion. Like Bediako, Choy employs autobiography

28. Choy, *Ancestral Feeling*, 16.
29. Sanneh, *Whose Religion Is Christianity?*, 22–23, as cited in Choy, *Ancestral Feeling*, 16.
30. Choy, *Ancestral Feeling*, 20.
31. Choy, *Ancestral Feeling*, 21.

in the form of her own religious genealogy, as a different method of doing history and, in practice, theology as well. Her project is "to discover whether Western Christian heritage can be anything other than an impenetrable historical chain to which I shall be forever late ... [through] embedding my own narrative and my own self as the very site of these histories."[32] Choy asks whether she should understand her spiritual heritage as that which has been grafted into the branch of Western Christianity. She does this by centering her own faith heritage instead of the Western tradition. In the end, Choy finds that "I destabilize 'the presence of the tap root, the canon, the standard, the patented,' and highlight instead the entangled web of personal relationships and experiences which have served to cement the tap root, canon, standard and patented in my life."[33] If one substitute's Choy's vocabulary of "heritage" with "tradition," then what she speaks of is a Western Christian tradition that she as a Canadian and British Chinese woman can claim as her own. That is, in the twenty-first century she can claim to be a native of the Western Christian tradition rather than a foreigner to it.

Choy believes the West relinquished any monopolistic claims to its Christian traditions through its missionary efforts, so Christians of color today can rightfully claim these traditions as their own spiritual and cultural heritage. Colonialism's legacy complicates this, yet even then Choy believes colonialism's impact can be overstated. For example, she cites John Coffey's observation that "Protestant Dissenting traditions have enjoyed disproportionate cultural influence across the Anglophone world, and were dispersed around the globe by generations of Protestant missionaries and indigenous evangelists."[34] While certainly nonstate-sponsored Christians also engaged in imperial activities, the majority of the recent growth of world Christianity traces its historical roots to these dissenting traditions. Choy's religious heritage then includes the voices and contributions of the colonizer and the colonized. To make sense of this dual reality she draws from the Indian philosopher Jarava Mehta's concept of the fusion

32. Choy, *Ancestral Feeling*, 92.
33. Choy, *Ancestral Feeling*, 30.
34. Coffey, introduction to *The Post-Reformation Era 1559–1689*, 34, as quoted in Choy, *Ancestral Feeling*, 47.

of horizons, one marked by loss and gain, in the "revoicing of the master's discourse in the cadences and timbres of the Black voice."[35] Choy describes her mother's singing of British hymns as "allowing my mother's fusion with the text to *change the way it is heard*."[36] She extends Bediako's understanding of the translated Bible into the vernacular to that of the Christian tradition. The Christian tradition also can be translated into the vernacular where it will be transformed by its new language and context. This new expression of the tradition will effectively communicate the gospel to its immediate context, and it will challenge more traditional expressions of Christianity to rethink the tradition. Choy comments, "The marginalized can often read and sing a work of Christian devotion better than anyone else."[37] A missional church should expect that its doctrine will take on new forms and produce new ideas unless it requires that its liturgy and theology be spoken in Latin or its modern equivalent, English.

Choy is not arguing that all Christians must embrace the Western theological tradition but simply that they can critically do so without committing racial, ethnic, or national betrayal. She argues against the false binary that to be a Christian and ethnically authentic one must renounce Western traditions. She writes, "The final barrier to break down—the one that needs our full resistance and protest—is the barrier that reserves 'high culture' for Western Christendom and a fervent, private, sincere Christianity for ethnic minorities."[38] While Christians of color may pride themselves in seeking a decolonized faith by rejecting the Western tradition, such thinking may keep them at the margins of Western cultural institutions and reinforce stereotypes. Choy's interest in "high culture" is not to be equated with the pursuit of status and wealth, but rather the resources that are associated with the Western Christian tradition. Choy clarifies, "In the same way that Chinese pianists have now become authoritative interpreters of Beethoven and Chopin, changing the way we experience Western cultural heritage, so it can be with Augustine and Aquinas."[39]

---

35. Choy, *Ancestral Feeling*, 113.
36. Choy, *Ancestral Feeling*, 113 (emphasis original).
37. Choy, *Ancestral Feeling*, 115.
38. Choy, *Ancestral Feeling*, 177.
39. Choy, *Ancestral Feeling*, 178.

Because of the spread of world Christianity, the West no longer possesses a monopoly on the Western Christian tradition. Thus, when Gustavo Gutiérrez constructs a theology and spirituality of liberation for the Latin American poor that claims "We drink from our own wells,"[40] that "our own" can include Bernard of Clairvaux, a twelfth-century French Catholic mystic who was a fierce advocate for the Crusades. Certainly having to sift the wheat from the chaff complicates the task of theology, but such is the vocation of the theologian in the twenty-first century.

What Is "Global Interpretation"?

As noted earlier, various cultures possess rich traditions of biblical interpretation in their own contexts that reception history studies will continue to make accessible to a wider audience. These include interpretations influenced by missionaries, so mapping contextual biblical interpretation involves engaging missiology, intercultural studies, and postcolonial studies. Certainly Bible translation, cross-cultural ministry, and contextual theology have been the domain of missionaries, but their insights have rarely impacted biblical studies. For some time, missionaries used insights from cultural anthropology to compare and contrast what they conceived of as assumptions between that of the Bible, Western cultures, and other cultures.[41] The American Kenneth Bailey's work on Jesus's parables is one of the few studies that tries to read the Bible intentionally with the use of "standard critical tools of Western scholarship in combination with cultural insights gained from ancient literature, contemporary peasants, and Oriental versions."[42]

The sea change in contextual biblical interpretation corresponds with the growth of the church in the Global South and East and the increase of Christians of color in the West. No longer would Euro-American scholars be at the forefront of contextual biblical interpretation, but rather Christians of color writing on behalf of their own communities. Philip Jenkins has chronicled the

40. Gutiérrez, *We Drink from Our Own Wells*.
41. Loewen, *Bible in Cross-Cultural Perspective*.
42. Bailey, *Poet & Peasant*, 29.

exponential growth of Indigenous forms of Christianity in Asia, Latin America, and Africa, and he has also gone on to describe the important role of the Bible in these regions. He observes that in the African and Asian church there is a great respect for the authority of the Bible, an appreciation of the Old Testament, an emphasis on supernatural and spiritual realities, and a belief in the Bible's relevance for real world concerns like poverty, famine, oppression, spiritual warfare, and persecution.[43] Jenkins has popularized what Sanneh and Walls have been describing for some time. They argue that once the Bible is translated into the vernacular, it becomes indigenized and embodied, and subsequent interpretations reflect the faith of the host culture.[44] The scales have tipped so that the majority of Christians live outside the West, and their Indigenous forms of biblical interpretation and theology are no longer marginal.

Scholars use the word *global* in multiple ways. It certainly does not always refer to the global church. Liberationist scholars sometimes appeal to the growth of Christianity among immigrant populations in the United States and the spread of Christianity in the Global South as justification for postcolonial and diasporic interpretive approaches,[45] but the majority of Christians in those regions are evangelical, Catholic, and Pentecostal. It is no secret that significant tensions and factions exist between churches in the Global West and South due to differences in sexual ethics, politics, economics, and other matters. The Western academy continues to influence education across the globe, and because of the prestige and influence of its universities, media, and publishing, it often sets the scholarly agenda. What may be published under the rubric of "Global Interpretation" by the West may not be representative of biblical interpretation across the globe. It may simply serve the interests of diversity initiatives in Western higher education, not Indigenous populations in much of the world. For example, Daniel Patte, in his introductory essay to the *Global Bible Commentary*, appeals to the growth of the global church

43. Jenkins, *New Faces of Christianity*.
44. Sanneh, *Translating the Message*, 13–96; Walls, *Missionary Movement*, 16–24, 43–50.
45. Segovia, "Interpreting Beyond Borders," 22–23.

as warrant for such a work.[46] Yet he also makes clear that the readings follow liberationist and postcolonial methodologies, and he says the book serves his pedagogical interests teaching diverse undergraduate and seminary students at Vanderbilt University. Evangelical and Pentecostal theologians tend to speak of "global or world Christianity" or "majority world theologies,"[47] and liberationist or postcolonial scholars, recognizing their scholarship is not representative of world Christianity, describe their writing as addressing "global perspectives" or "global concerns."

For readers in the West who are intent on incorporating evangelical theologies from the Global South and East into their own methodologies, it is worth considering why North American and European academics have long misrepresented these regions by ignoring or excluding their theologies. For example, in the 1970s Latin American theology was often mistakenly equated with liberation theology, and the theological contributions of Latin American evangelicals were completely overlooked.[48] It is difficult to determine precisely why both liberal and conservative scholars in the West ignore evangelical scholars from the Global South. The reasons likely vary but may include the following:

1. They are perceived as not producing original, legitimate, or robust scholarship.
2. They are too theologically conservative, particularly those representing evangelical and Pentecostal backgrounds.
3. They are too conservative socially, particularly in regard to sexual and gender ethics.
4. Their theologies and faith practices are at odds with Western norms.
5. They do not fit into traditional disciplinary categories.
6. They appear too exotic.
7. They complicate the identarian racial politics of the academy.

46. Patte, introduction to *Global Bible Interpretation*, xxi.
47. See, e.g., Dyrness and Kärkkäinen, *Global Dictionary of Theology*; Green, Pardue, and Yeo, *Majority World Theology*.
48. See Salinas, *Latin American Evangelical Theology*, 1–17; Kirkpatrick, *Gospel for the Poor*, 53–71.

Yet engagement with the Global South and East remains important for the present theological task if representation, participation, inclusion, community, and solidarity are important values. One out of four Christians in the world today is Pentecostal or charismatic,[49] and evangelical and charismatic communities comprise much of the world's religious poor. If one cares about the religious poor in the Global South, one must engage evangelical and charismatic Christianity.

Simon Chan asserts that "much of what the West knows as Asian theology consists largely of elitist accounts of what Asian theologians are saying, and elitist theologians seldom take grassroots Christianity seriously."[50] He goes on to criticize how Asian theology has been misrepresented by a narrow focus on a few elite theologians who represent the theology of Europe, not Asia.[51] Chan provides the example of C. S. Song, who "is frequently cited as an example of an Asian theologian. But in point of fact, his theology hardly qualifies as Asian."[52] Chan consistently refers to Asian theologians who promote liberationist hermeneutics as "elitist theologians." While it is unfair and inaccurate to group all theologians who espouse liberationist approaches into a monolith, a consistent stream of criticism is leveled against some liberation theologians not merely at an intellectual level but also at an *ethical* level. In chapter 3 I described Marcella Althaus-Reid's criticism of classic and popular Latin American liberation theologians for romanticizing the poor in order to construct theologies of the poor and capitalize on the North Atlantic academic industry. R. S. Sugirtharajah describes how Latin American theology led to the development of identity-based theologies on a global scale. Given their genealogy, it is worth asking whether liberation theologies that developed after the rise of Latin American theology also, to borrow a phrase from Althaus-Reid, "went to Disneyland" by constructing artificial theologies of the poor and marginalized to serve North American and European academic interests. Chan certainly believes academic Asian theologies are guilty of doing so.

49. Granberg-Michaelson, *Future Faith*, 88.
50. Chan, *Grassroots Asian Theology*, 7.
51. Sugirtharajah has similarly observed how these theologians are transplants from Europe.
52. Chan, *Grassroots Asian Theology*, 21.

It seems only Asian liberation theologies that followed the model of classic Latin American liberation theology were in demand in the academic marketplace of the late twentieth century, and without any other competitors they monopolized the term "Asian Theology." Some academics professionally profited from these actions and gained the ability to advocate for greater diversity and inclusion in the academy. Meanwhile an inaccurate depiction of ecclesial communities in the non-West persisted in mainline traditions, while some conservative Christians in the non-West grew suspicious of contextual theologies and turned to fundamentalist forms of Christianity. Given the history of academic contextual theology's development, a fair question to ask of contextual theologies is whether they are, in Althaus-Reid's term, "theme park theologies" and to what degree they, along with other Western theologies, have colonized the intellectual lives of non-Western Christians. Chan offers the reminder that "ecclesial experience constitutes the primary theology (*theologia prima*) of the church."[53] Thus, Christian contextual theologies are not validated through peer review in the Western academy, but rather through their practice by local congregations.

A wide range of contextual theologies exist, including highly sophisticated forms done by academics, grassroots and populist versions that often exist solely in oral traditions, and liberationist forms that are constructed by scholars, Christians from lower classes, or some combination of both. The interest in these so-called global theologies and biblical interpretations in both the majority world and the West has led to the proliferation of contextual interpretations. These studies may frustrate traditional biblical scholars because of their abundance, unfamiliarity, and diversity. They do not fit neatly into a particular step of biblical exegesis, such as "historical analysis" or "application," and they cannot be summarized in a chapter devoted to "African interpretation" or the like in a volume on biblical hermeneutics. Contextual interpretation defies the traditional taxonomies within the discipline of biblical studies, so attempts to reduce it to a "method" or "exegetical step" misrepresent it.

53. Chan, *Grassroots Asian Theology*, 15–16.

Western and non-Western scholars have attempted to create dialogue for the sake of mutual learning. An early example is Mark Branson and C. René Padilla's *Conflict and Context: Hermeneutics in the Americas*, which includes papers presented by North American and Latin American biblical scholars, as well as their dialogue over a range of topics. In a more recent study, scholars from Europe and Africa presented their different approaches to biblical interpretation, followed by respondents to the question, "What does Africa have to say to Europe and Europe to Africa about the bible?"[54] The exchange included both "exegesis" and "actualization"—that is, exploring meanings within the world of the text as well as the application and recontextualization of it. Another form of contextual scholarship would be Europeans or North Americans compiling the interpretations of the same biblical passage by scholars from Africa, Latin America, and Asia for the sake of comparison and learning between cultures.[55] Justin Ukpong describes the differences between Western and African hermeneutics in the following manner: "I designate classical Western Bible reading methodologies as *intellectualist*. By that I mean that they professedly seek objective truth as interpretive interest, and profess to employ a universal perspective. . . . By contrast, however, African readings are *existential and pragmatic* in nature, and *contextual* in approach. They are interested in relating the biblical message to contemporary and existential questions, and lay no claim to a universal perspective."[56] Ukpong's critique is that the differences between Western and African readings are not based on geography and culture but rather class; they represent the different interests of elite intellectuals and ordinary readers. Western academics are eager to facilitate studies with "ordinary readers" in South America and Africa and among the "damned" in North America,[57] but not the ordinary reader in the United States or Europe. In this approach, Western biblical scholarship is irrelevant to the non-West,

54. De Wit, Snoek, and West, introduction to *African and European Readers*, ix.
55. Dietrich and Luz, *Bible in a World Context*; Pope-Levison and Levison, *Return to Babel*.
56. Ukpong, "Inculturation Hermeneutics," 17 (emphasis original).
57. Ekblad, *Reading the Bible*.

and it fails to serve the church in the West. Instead, it serves the interests of the academy, not the actual needs of ordinary people.

The most prolific contextual biblical scholarship from an intercultural perspective has come from evangelical Christians in the Global South and East. Much of this is published by Langham Partnership, a ministry begun by John Stott dedicated to resourcing the majority world church. Thus far it has published seventy-two theological monographs as well as one-volume commentaries on the entire Bible for Africa, South Asia, Eastern Europe, Latin America, and the Middle East. Two volumes on Old Testament books have been written in the Africa Bible Commentary Series and fourteen Old Testament volumes in the Asia Bible Commentary Series. Works on African biblical hermeneutics, Old Testament biblical interpretation in Asian contexts, Bible translation, preaching, contextual theology, and contextual ethics have been published. Latin American evangelicals have long wrestled with contextual matters of theology and biblical interpretation due in part to the challenge of liberation theology, and they have produced substantial scholarship of their own.[58] In North America, evangelical theologians and biblical scholars have referred to these interpretations as representative of the "majority world" as a critique of both liberal and conservative Western Christianity.[59] Evangelical biblical scholars of color in the West are navigating their bicultural status alongside their transnational ties, so their context includes global concerns as well as the struggles of being racial minorities in the West. It seems that these publications may be genuinely contextual given that they are primarily aimed to serve ecclesial communities of color rather than the interests of the Western academy.

Conclusion

What is common to all forms of contextual interpretation, whether liberationist or intercultural, is that biblical interpretation is no longer viewed as an objective method to determine historical meanings.

58. See Heaney, *Contextual Theology*.
59. E.g., Green, Pardue, and Yeo, *Majority World Theology*; Yeh and Tiénou, *Majority World Theologies*.

Historical criticism, or the "historical-grammatical method," has been chastened and sometimes displaced altogether. Rather than strive for critical distance between reader and text throughout the process of exegesis and then conclude with reflections on own one's context, contextual interpretation reverses the order. Now readers often identify, reflect on, and possibly critique their context as the first step in biblical interpretation. How interpreters reflect on their contexts differs based on the goals of interpretation. Liberationist interpreters typically use social-scientific and postcolonial methods to understand their own context and will then apply these methods to biblical interpretation. Evangelical interpreters in non-Western contexts are increasingly incorporating Indigenous contextual theologies and cultural resources to understand themselves as well as interpret the Bible.

What will be the future of biblical scholarship when biblical scholars live far removed from the contexts of those who actually read the Bible? While the Bible may continue to serve an iconic role in Europe and the United States, the actual reading of the Bible is diminishing in the West while the importance and relevance of the Bible continues to grow in the Global South and East. Hans de Wit admits, "Someone who comes from the Brazilian CEBs [Christian Base Communities] and looks at the place of the bible in the Dutch context gets an ice-cold bath."[60] In instances where Western and non-Western scholars engage in substantive dialogue over biblical interpretation, they discuss much more than hermeneutical and textual matters. Scholars from both Europe and Africa agree that authentic intercultural interpretation is going to require economic, political, and social rearrangements between communities. Scholars will have to engage this reality if they want to produce scholarship relevant to the Bible's diverse readership in the present and future.

60. De Wit, "Exegesis and Contextuality," 17. He goes on to cite statistics that in the Netherlands only 13 percent of the people regularly read the Bible.

6

Models of Contextual and Theological Interpretation

<figure>⸙</figure>

This chapter provides several examples of contextual and theological interpretation that I believe serve multicultural congregations well. The interpreters chosen represent a range of methodologies, sociocultural contexts, and theological backgrounds, and they engage various biblical texts and pastoral concerns. Represented are both theologians and biblical scholars, readings of Old and New Testaments, and scholars based in the Global South and West.

Kwame Bediako and the Bible as Contextual Interpretation

Kwame Bediako provides a theological justification for interpreting the Bible contextually in his essay, "Biblical Exegesis in the African Context." He begins by citing Clement of Alexandria: "It was not alien to the inspiration of God, who gave the prophecy, also to produce the translation, and make it as it were, Greek prophecy."[1] In doing so, Bediako anchors his argument in the patristic tradition. Clement's comment is significant because it extends divine inspiration

---

1. *Stromata* 1.22.149, as quoted in Bediako, "Biblical Exegesis," 15.

beyond the original Hebrew text of the Scriptures to the Greek translation. Bediako is well aware that the early church primarily read the Greek translation of the Jewish Scriptures such that the Septuagint can be referred to as "the first Bible of the church."[2] He cites Andrew Walls's claim that the pre-Christian translation of the Septuagint served a crucial role in the development of an Indigenous Christianity since it functioned as "a direction indicator for the encounter of many peoples in their subsequent interaction with the Christian faith."[3] As a "direction indicator," Bediako says the Greek translation "contributed to the shape of the Scriptures themselves. Thus the Septuagint brought Christian theology to a position from which it was not possible to retreat."[4]

Bediako highlights the fact that the Christian Bible is a translation from the original and that biblical insights found in the Greek translation served a formative role in early Christian theology. He cites the New Testament scholar Henry Barclay Swete—"The New Testament would have been a widely different book had it been written by authors who knew the Old Testament only in the original"[5]— and then he explores how the Septuagint impacted the theology of the New Testament. Bediako examines two well-known examples of New Testament authors making unique theological claims based on the Greek text of the Jewish Scriptures. In Matthew 1:22's quotation of Isaiah 7:14 and Acts 15:16–18's quotation of Amos 9:11–12, the New Testament teaching depends directly on textual aspects unique to the Greek translation. Bediako examines these texts to provide biblical warrant for Lamin Sanneh's thesis that translation exerted a dual force in early Christianity: "One was to resolve to relativise its Judaic roots. . . . The other was to destigmatise Gentile culture and adopt that culture as the natural extension of the life of the new religion."[6] Bediako observes that the canonical Scripture itself is a translation, the early church primarily read this translation, and the translation did not adulterate the gospel but made distinct

2. Müller, *First Bible*, 126, as cited in Bediako, "Biblical Exegesis," 15.
3. Walls, *Missionary Movement*, 35, as quoted in Bediako, "Biblical Exegesis," 15.
4. Bediako, "Biblical Exegesis," 15.
5. Swete, *Old Testament in Greek*, 404, as quoted in Bediako, "Biblical Exegesis," 15.
6. Sanneh, *Translating the Message*, 1, as quoted in Bediako, "Biblical Exegesis," 16.

contributions to its understanding. If such was the case in the early church, Bediako concludes that the contemporary church can and ought to view translations as "the natural extension"[7] of early Christianity.

This understanding of translation leads to a significant shift in the task of biblical interpretation. Rather than viewing Scripture as confined to a specific text, Bediako believes "it is possible to think of the Scriptures also as context, a context that the reader (or hearer) may enter and so actually participate in their world of meaning and experience."[8] Divine inspiration thus extends beyond the original texts to include the modern translations. It did not stop with the ancient authors but continues in the lives of contemporary readers attempting to make sense of it in varying contexts. Bediako writes, "If there is any merit in the concept of the Scriptures as also context, that persons of varied cultural backgrounds can enter and participate in, bringing their own cultural worlds with them, then it can also be said that the exegesis of biblical texts may not be taken as completed when one has established meanings in Hebrew, Aramaic, and Greek. Instead, the process needs to continue into all possible languages in which biblical faith is received, mediated, and expressed."[9] Rather than having interpreters set aside their own cultural concerns in the attempt to seek objectivity, Bediako considers such concerns essential to the task of interpretation. By appealing to the history of the Bible itself, Bediako demonstrates that interpretation is not complete until the Bible is translated into contemporary cultural forms.

Once the translation of the ancient Scriptures is also considered to be divinely inspired, then the ancient versions are no longer viewed as the sole texts for Scripture study. Bediako closely examines the Twi understanding of *logos* in John 1:1, as well as the Akan understanding of the spiritual realm in Exodus 15:11, Psalm 86:8, and Exodus 20:1–3. His purpose for studying these translations is not to determine how closely they align with the original versions. Instead, he engages in a participatory form of interpretation where both the ancient text and the contemporary translation serve as

7. Sanneh, *Translating the Message*, 1, as quoted in Bediako, "Biblical Exegesis," 16.
8. Bediako, "Biblical Exegesis," 18.
9. Bediako, "Biblical Exegesis," 18.

vehicles for Christian teaching. If Scripture is also context, then translation becomes text. Biblical interpretation then looks to the ancient text as well as to its translated forms to reveal God's truth. The ancient text is not a superior form of revelation, nor does it possess a monopoly on Christian truth. Bediako writes, "Such an enhanced appreciation of the exegetical significance of the translated Scriptures will be an effective response to what appears to be a sort of 'Bible deism' that suggests that after God spoke in Hebrew, Aramaic, and Greek, he ceased to speak to humanity in any other language, a presumption that is firmly contradicted by the continuous communicative thrust of the Scriptures themselves."[10] Although Bediako does not cite Acts 2, his insights affirm the Holy Spirit's work initiated at Pentecost.

By locating divine inspiration beyond ancient texts to modern translations, Bediako expands the locus of biblical authority. If God can speak meaningfully and perhaps in unique ways through modern translations, then the authority of historical biblical interpretation is relativized. Biblical interpretation expands to include its reception, with the understanding that God may speak new insights through ongoing translation.

K. K. Yeo and Cross-Cultural Interpretation

Few scholars have devoted their careers to cross-cultural biblical interpretation and theology in the manner of K. K. Yeo. While his context and focus are Christian Chinese biblical interpretation, he has always written to enrich and expand cross-cultural interpretation at a global level. Yeo believes the goal of cross-cultural interpretation is to "allow one's culture and the biblical interpretation to interact, differentiate, and be mutually transformed."[11] His methods include philosophical hermeneutics, biblical exegesis, sociocultural analysis, and global theology, and his understanding of language, rhetoric, metaphor, and culture is informed by Hans-Georg Gadamer, Paul Ricoeur, Kenneth Burke, Clifford Geertz, I. A.

---

10. Bediako, "Biblical Exegesis," 22.
11. Yeo, *Jerusalem*, 36.

Richards, and Max Black. While Yeo recognizes the practicalities in the division of labor between the academy and the church, he rejects "the privileging and prioritizing of biblical interpretations in the dualistic form of historical-academic over that of spiritual-practical mentality"[12] that his Western theological training often assumes. For him theology is a practice of spiritual formation that involves contemplation and is to be done for the sake of practical mission in the world. Yeo views theology as a dynamic enterprise, which therefore "needs to live and work in the *dynamic tensions* that exist between the word of God and the community of believers, between biblical and systematic theologies, and between exegesis and homiletics."[13] Cross-cultural interpretation requires interdisciplinary engagement and transgresses the boundaries between the church and academy.

Yeo is willing to critique both Western and Chinese forms of biblical interpretation and theology, yet his writing is more constructive in nature. He admits, "If there is in these chapters an irenic tone and the desire to promote understanding and acceptance, my intent is not to be patronizing, but to relate my humbling journey and the implications for our responsibility as Bible readers."[14] His irenic tone and humble posture stem from a desire for cross-cultural understanding and global ecumenism. As a bicultural and transnational person, Yeo possesses first-hand knowledge of the strengths and weaknesses of multiple cultures and societies. While he finds value in various Chinese and Western readings of the Bible, he recognizes that every culture possesses deficiencies, and the consequences of failing to address these inadequacies can be dire. For example, he is well aware of the influence of anti-Semitism in twentieth-century German biblical scholarship and the impact of anti-Arab and anti-Palestinian sentiments on Zionist theologies. Yeo writes, "The urgent issue with which I am struggling is the meta-critical principle within cross-cultural and critical readings of the Bible, so that contextual readings would not lead us to fall into the trap of nationalism."[15] So while several of Yeo's

12. Yeo, *Jerusalem*, 314.
13. Yeo, *Jerusalem*, 5 (emphasis original).
14. Yeo, *Jerusalem*, 310.
15. Yeo, *Jerusalem*, 315.

works are devoted to interpreting the Bible in a Chinese context,[16] much of his scholarship focuses on cross-cultural hermeneutics[17] and global theology.[18] His Christian Chinese interpretations of Scripture take the form of comparative linguistic and religious readings as well as political theological interpretations. For example, Yeo compares Paul's notions of "Torah and Spirit" with Confucian understandings of "Li and Ren,"[19] and he reads Isaiah 5:1–7 and 27:2–6 in light of the events of Tiananmen Square.[20] For Yeo the "hermeneutical circle of scriptural criticism—reading Scripture through the lens of culture—also includes culture criticism—reading culture through the lens of Scripture."[21]

Fundamental to Yeo's biblical and theological methodology is the recognition that "Christianity does not believe in a revealed language; we believe in a revealed message in changing space and time."[22] He finds theological warrant for cross-cultural biblical interpretation from Paul's teaching on Jewish-gentile relationships in the book of Galatians. Paul's teaching on the centrality of Christ and freedom for cultural expression serves as a paradigm for ongoing cross-cultural theological reflection. Yeo writes, "Christ's ontology enables 'every tribe and language and people and nation' (Rev. 5:9; 7:9; 13:7; 14:6; cf. Acts 2:1–13) to be 'fully Christian and fully Chinese' (or fully Christian and fully Jewish, likewise fully Christian and fully gentile) in their *theologizing*, which constitutes part of Christian worship. Cross-cultural biblical interpretation intends to make that eschatological, aesthetic movement, 'Jesus Christ is the Reality that makes all realities, cultures, and meaning-systems true, beautiful, and good.'"[23]

His understandings of the doctrines of Christology and eschatology serve as the theological warrant for his cross-cultural biblical

---

16. Yeo, *Rhetorical Interaction*; Yeo, *Jerusalem*; Yeo, *Chairman Mao Meets the Apostle Paul*; Yeo, *Musing with Confucius and Paul*; Yeo, *Oxford Handbook of the Bible in China*.

17. Cosgrove, Weiss, and Yeo, *Cross-Cultural Paul*.

18. Green, Pardue, and Yeo, *Majority World Theology*.

19. Yeo, *Jerusalem*, 137–64.

20. Yeo, *Jerusalem*, 242–67.

21. Yeo, *Jerusalem*, 29.

22. Yeo, *Jerusalem*, 21.

23. Yeo, *Jerusalem*, 52 (emphasis original).

hermeneutic. In regard to Christology, Yeo claims that "only Jesus is normative, and no Christology is absolute,"[24] so he holds to the authority of Jesus as presented in Scripture but acknowledges the limitations of precisely understanding the identity and significance of this figure. Thus, he believes the contemporary church can conceive of Christologies beyond Chalcedon, not because its creedal formulation was flawed, but because it lacks comprehensiveness. In the richness and variety of the global church's witness, Yeo sees an opportunity to practice a true catholicity that captures the expansive testimony of the fourfold Gospels and Pauline Christology. Yeo will interact with creeds, tradition, and notable theologians, but he grants them a relative authority in light of Scripture's witness.

Yeo describes his biblical and theological method as a process that involves three steps:

1. The rhetorical plane, the linguistic world of the biblical author
2. The plane of biblical exegesis, the reader's concern for the historical meaning of the text
3. A modern interpreter's understanding of the first two planes, an interaction with one's modern audience, and the configuration of the message

Yeo describes the rhetorical plane as triangulating the signified (reality), the signifier (language), and the biblical author (rhetor as language user). He finds this interpretive step complex since in his case it involves constantly translating between not only the Hebrew, Greek, and Chinese words but also the worlds they signify. For example, translating the Greek term *logos* in John 1 with the Chinese word *dao* raises the question whether the word suggests the Daoist cosmic dao or the Confucianist notion of dao as a certain character or person. In the second step, Yeo seeks to understand the rhetorical communication of the biblical author in relation to the contextual issues of the modern interpreter. In the third step, Yeo envisions an interaction between what he terms the kairotic message of the text, the modern interpreter, and the modern audience. This hermeneutic

24. Yeo, "Biblical Christologies," 216.

operates with the theological assumption "that behind the human writers of the biblical texts, is the divine author whose meaning must be so rich, multilayered, and expansive that only his Spirit can: (1) not only incarnate linguistically in the first languages as well as in translated vernaculars; (2) but also enlighten modern interpreters in our languages and understandings so that the biblical text continues to show its sacred power to speak God's message across space and time."[25]

Gustavo Gutiérrez's Theological and Contextual Commentary

Gustavo Gutiérrez's *On Job: God-Talk and the Suffering of the Innocent* defies the categorizations of academic theology. It is biblical commentary, a work on theological method, and an exercise in Christian spirituality, all directed toward the pastoral needs of the Latin American context. Engaging a wide range of subjects is not new to Gutiérrez, whose other works engage the topics of theology, biblical study, and spirituality.[26] What is perhaps significant or unique to *On Job* is that he synthesizes these concerns in the form of a theological and contextual commentary on the book of Job. Gutiérrez intentionally fuses genres because he believes it is precisely this interdisciplinary engagement that is required for formation of faith in Latin America. He admits in his introduction, "I shall adopt a standpoint that is dear to me, that of the connection, and even the identity, between theological methodology and spirituality."[27] Theological method is the overriding concern for this work, so *On Job* represents a different way of doing theology, reading the Bible, and practicing the Christian faith. Gutiérrez's intellectual conversation partners span these disciplines. He engages historical-critical biblical scholars, classic and liberation theologians, and Latin American intellectuals. While he clearly writes for the Latin American context, Gutiérrez's audience is global, so although his readers may not share his sociopolitical context, he

25. Yeo, *Jerusalem*, 21.
26. Gutiérrez, *Theology of Liberation*; Gutiérrez, *God of Life*; Gutiérrez, *We Drink from Our Own Wells*.
27. Gutiérrez, *On Job*, xviii.

believes his theological methodology ought to be embraced by all Christians.

Gutiérrez goes to great lengths to define his writing as *theo*logy, the study of God. This move is likely in response to criticisms that he is overly concerned with horizontal relationships and does not sufficiently address one's vertical relationship with God. He opens his commentary by calling attention to the fact that Thomas Aquinas's *Summa Theologiae* begins with the apophatic claim, "We cannot know what God is but only what God is not."[28] By doing so Gutiérrez situates himself squarely within the Romans Catholic ecclesial tradition, a tradition that he believes is expansive enough to allow for contextual theological methods. He finds that the mystery of God, which he understands as the validation for a contemplative spirituality, is "a theme that is central both to classic theology and to theology of liberation."[29] Gutiérrez's second methodological move in the introduction is to identify the context for his theology to demonstrate that, while the commentary's concern is the knowledge of God, it equally takes seriously the conditions in which the study of God occurs. Both concerns are illustrated in the question central to the commentary: "How are we to talk about a God who is revealed as love in a situation characterized by poverty and oppression?"[30]

In liberation theology, poverty and oppression are inseparable, the first being the result of the later, so that the contextual question "is not with the 'evil of guilt' but rather with the 'evil of misfortune,' the evil suffered by the innocent."[31] Gutiérrez believes that the suffering of Amerindians continues in the present among the poor in Latin America and elsewhere in the world, and that their suffering resembles what Jesus Christ experienced. He believes that evangelical faith, the death and resurrection of Christ, comprises the "center of the world," and then he conflates the sufferings of the poor and Christ so that together they encompass the center of his theology. From the interpretation of the early fathers to Karl Barth, he appeals to church tradition that sees Job as a type of Christ for

28. Thomas Aquinas, *Summa Theologiae*, I, 9, 3, as cited in Gutiérrez, *On Job*, xi.
29. Gutiérrez, *On Job*, xiii.
30. Gutiérrez, *On Job*, xiv.
31. Gutiérrez, *On Job*, xv.

hermeneutical warrant to see Job as a Christ figure and also as a representative of the suffering poor. Gutiérrez does not construct his hermeneutic inductively from reading Job, and he acknowledges that the book's teachings run against the grain of liberation theology. Yet this is not a problem for him since, in accordance with the claims of liberation theology, he never claims objectivity or disinterest but rather acknowledges that "to read the Bible from the standpoint of our deepest and most pressing concerns . . . has also in fact been the practice of the Christian community throughout its history."[32] For Gutiérrez, the Christian tradition provides him theological warrant to read Job with a liberation hermeneutic.

Gutiérrez is attentive to the literary structure of Job and identifies two important shifts in the book that contribute to its overall message:

> The first occurs when, at the instigation of his friends, he broadens his perspective, abandons his initial narrow position, and realizes that the issue here is not simply the suffering of one individual. The real issue, he sees, is the suffering and injustice that mark the lives of the poor. Those who believe in God must therefore try to lighten the burden of the poor by helping them and practicing solidarity with them. The speeches of God occasion the second shift: Job now understands that the world of justice must be located within the broad but demanding horizon of freedom that is formed by the gratuitousness of God's love.[33]

Gutiérrez organizes his commentary according to these shifts, dividing it into three parts where part 1, "The Wager," sets the stage for his main argument. Part 2, "The Language of Prophecy," interprets the debate between Job and his friends and reflects on the struggles of the poor in Gutiérrez's context. In keeping with Gutierrez's commitment to both spirituality and a liberative theology, part 3, "The Language of Contemplation," probes the depths of God's gratuitousness in Job's engagement with God. In these movements Gutierrez demonstrates this commitment to the horizontal and vertical dimensions of Christian faith, and to both activism and contemplation.

32. Gutiérrez, *On Job*, xvii.
33. Gutiérrez, *On Job*, 16.

The hermeneutical decision to interpret Job not as an individual but rather communally as representative of the poor significantly impacts Gutiérrez's interpretation of the book. The debate among Job's friends is universalized to extend to the poor and marginalized. The teaching of Job no longer deals merely with theodicy but now examines social ethics. Readers who would typically identify with Job, if they are not among the world's poor, must identify instead as one of Job's friends. Job defends his innocence, yet his friends argue that his suffering is justified due to his wrongdoing. Readers must examine their attitudes and actions toward the poor and examine whether they blame the poor for their poverty. Gutiérrez highlights the historic connections Christians have made between the retribution principle and capitalism, noting that "in the course of the history of the Church certain tendencies in the Christian world have repeatedly given new life to the ethical doctrine that regards wealth as God's reward to the honest and the hard-working, and poverty as God's punishment to the sinful and the lazy."[34]

Gutiérrez demonstrates that care for the poor is an integral part of the message of Job. In chapter 5 he examines Job 24:2–14, a lengthy passage that describes the wicked as attaining wealth through corrupt and cruel practices of exploiting and stealing from the poor. Gutiérrez highlights the speech of Eliphaz, who in Job 22:4–9 identifies Job's "unlimited sins" (22:5) as the exploitation and oppression of the poor. Gutiérrez devotes his final chapter of part 2 to Job 29–31, where Job provides a lengthy monologue in which he responds to the accusations of Eliphaz and his other companions. Gutiérrez observes that Job defends his innocence and righteousness by recalling how he sought the liberation of the poor and opposed the exploitative actions of the wicked (29:12–17). In all these passages, poverty is the direct result of injustice and oppression so that one cannot speak about the poor without addressing oppression. These teachings support Gutiérrez's claim that the central concern of Job is "is not with the 'evil of guilt' but rather with the 'evil of misfortune,' the evil suffered by the innocent."[35] Both Job and God assume the title "father of the

---

34. Gutiérrez, *On Job*, 22.
35. Gutiérrez, *On Job*, xv.

poor" (see Job 29:16; cf. Ps. 68:5) so that Gutiérrez can conclude, "To give to the needy is therefore to give to God: 'He who is kind to the poor lends to the Lord' (Prov. 19:17)."[36]

Even as Gutiérrez affirms the validity and importance of the book's prophetic speech against injustice, he acknowledges that it is inadequate and in the last movement of his commentary addresses the role of contemplation. Gutiérrez recognizes that Job's quest for justice is not merely a social, economic, or political matter but is fundamentally a spiritual struggle with God. He says the speeches of Job resemble the laments in Psalm 73:2–14 and Lamentations 3:1–9, so although Job complains to his friends (Job 19:21–22), ultimately his complaint is directed toward God. God is the one who possesses the capacity to address Job's complaint of unjust suffering. Gutiérrez interprets the redeemer (gō'ēl; 19:25) in Job's appeal as none other than God. Gutiérrez acknowledges that even though God is Job's liberator, Job's complaint of unjust suffering is not resolved. Instead, the book affirms the mystery of God. God's speeches at the close of the book affirm two freedoms: the freedom of God and the freedom of humans that result in suffering in the world. Gutiérrez writes, "Job's freedom finds expression in his complaints and rebellion; God's freedom finds expression in the gratuitousness of the divine love that refuses to be confined within a system of predictable rewards and punishments."[37] Gutiérrez believes the book of Job does not invalidate the importance of justice but subsumes it under the gratuitousness of God. He grounds his theology according to this truth so that "the ultimate basis for the privileged position of the poor is not in the poor themselves but in God, in the gratuitousness and universality of God's *agapeic* love."[38] Gutiérrez concludes his commentary by affirming a threefold commitment for his community to "find our own route amid the present sufferings and hopes of the poor of Latin America, to analyze its course with the requisite historical effectiveness, and, above all, to compare it anew with the word of God."[39]

36. Gutiérrez, *On Job*, 40.
37. Gutiérrez, *On Job*, 80.
38. Gutiérrez, *On Job*, 94.
39. Gutiérrez, *On Job*, 102.

What one observes from Gutiérrez is a reflexive engagement between his context and interests and the Scriptures. He by no means reads his liberation theology into every text of Job, dismissing interpretations that might challenge his preexisting views. His commentary ends, like the book of Job, with tensions in his theology that are not resolved by intellectual argument but through engagement in spiritual practices. Gutiérrez embraces a traditional interpretation of the book by arguing that God's justice is subsumed under God's freedom and that humans must submit to the mystery of God. A unique contribution of his commentary, certainly borne out of Gutiérrez's interests, is highlighting Job's abundant teaching on justice toward the poor. His decision to equate Job with the poor is a bold and provocative interpretive decision, and one that leads to a stimulating reading of the book.

Love Sechrest and a Methodology for Multicultural Interpretation

Love Sechrest's 2022 book, *Race & Rhyme: Rereading the New Testament*, is one of the most comprehensive works on multicultural biblical interpretation. She provides an extensive explanation for her contextual hermeneutic and applies her interpretive approach across the New Testament, not simply to a few select texts. Through both its substantive methodology and biblical interpretation, *Race & Rhyme* offers a robust hermeneutical model for readers. The work is academic, pedagogical, and personal as it contains Sechrest's extensive work in New Testament studies and African American biblical interpretation, insights gained from years of teaching the subject to seminary students, and reflections on her move away from progressive evangelicalism to womanist theology in the midst of a racial reckoning in the United States. Even for those who may not be interested in the topics of womanist theology, race, and New Testament studies, the book models the practice of contextual biblical interpretation to different contexts, topics, and texts.

Sechrest introduces her methodology as "associative hermeneutics," which is a method based on identifying the "rhyme" between contemporary issues and biblical texts. She acknowledges that employing analogy as a method for biblical moral reflection is not new;

what is distinct about her approach is the associations drawn. In contrast to Richard Hays, who places cross, community, and new creation as focal images of New Testament ethics,[40] Sechrest chooses to "center the womanist values of liberation for Black women and other marginalized communities."[41] The focus of her New Testament reading is on how "intergroup conflict, ethnoracial tension, and power dynamics in the New Testament promotes liberative reflection on race relations in contemporary life."[42] Sechrest is committed to respecting the integrity of the ancient text's teaching, refusing to "collapse the ancient narratives in the Bible into the much more complicated problems in modern society."[43] When drawing analogies, she is quick to identify differences between the ancient text and contemporary issue. Sechrest believes ancient historical contexts ought to be taken seriously, so she does not criticize historical criticism for being biased, hegemonic, or Eurocentric as other contextual interpreters sometimes do. Instead, she finds that historical interpretations "help illuminate the distance between the ancient artifact and the modern condition in a way that allows readers to improvise on biblical harmonies."[44] Since the historical interpretation is not the sole or normative reading of Scripture, historical criticism is not viewed as hegemonic but rather as an important tool in the interpretive process. Sechrest believes that readers should extend the same courtesies to ancient authors that she would want extended to her writings. Since she views the Bible as "coauthored by people constrained by culture and limited horizons,"[45] historical study is essential since its ancient form provides the basis for which to draw associations to contemporary culture, both like and unlike. Sechrest says it is impossible to determine "timeless and transcendent principles"[46] from the Bible since the text is always culturally conditioned, so biblical interpretation needs to take account of the historic differences between contemporary readers and ancient

40. Hays, *Moral Vision*.
41. Sechrest, *Race & Rhyme*, 3n5.
42. Sechrest, *Race & Rhyme*, 3.
43. Sechrest, *Race & Rhyme*, 3.
44. Sechrest, *Race & Rhyme*, 18.
45. Sechrest, *Race & Rhyme*, 19.
46. Sechrest, *Race & Rhyme*, 29.

texts. Determining the "biblical situation" and "biblical response" to a text is Sechrest's first stage in the process of interpretation, and to achieve these ends Sechrest utilizes traditional historical-critical methods.

Race & Rhyme is part autobiographical, as Sechrest recounts her own intellectual journey toward a womanist theology. She describes how early on she attempted to read the Bible with a hermeneutic of trust but found that she experienced a growing "distaste for trying to 'save' a text and make excuses for it."[47] She eventually concluded that the Bible contains "illiberative" texts. She considers the Bible to be divinely superintended in its writing, important for contemporary ethics, and offering a message of liberation. Yet because its ethical vision is limited by its ancient cultural context, Sechrest says the Bible should be taken seriously but not literally. By this she means that contemporary persons are "better positioned to read it as morally responsible agents embedded in different cultures but struggling with similar problems that arise from the human condition."[48] She acknowledges that some biblical authors embrace slavery, genocide, ethnocentrism, and misogyny and says such teachings ought to be rejected. She also agrees with the enterprise of historical criticism such that "however much I may read myself into the stories of the text, these stores are not, in fact, my own."[49] For Sechrest it is important to maintain the cultural distance between the contemporary reader and the ancient text. Yet it is in the interaction between the contemporary and ancient culture that Sechrest says the Bible can speak toward liberative concerns.

The contemporary lens Sechrest uses to engage the ancient text of the Bible is womanist theology. Womanist theology centers the experience and concerns of Black women, and in doing so it shares resonances and dissonances with both feminist theology and Black theology. Sechrest acknowledges that womanist biblical interpretation was nearly nonexistent during her doctoral studies in the early 2000s, but since then it has developed a robust tradition. Scholars such as Renita Weems have spoken of how the combination of sexism,

47. Sechrest, *Race & Rhyme*, xii.
48. Sechrest, *Race & Rhyme*, 19.
49. Sechrest, *Race & Rhyme*, 18.

racism, and classism uniquely impacts Black women. Wil Gafney
explores the use of the "sanctified imagination" when reading texts in
the Black church, Nyasha Junior describes the longstanding engagement of African women with the Bible, and Mitzi Smith and Kelly
Brown Douglas identify the areas of oppression womanist theology
resists and the liberative themes they embrace. In addition to describing womanist theology, Sechrest describes her understanding of race
relations, defining terms such as ethnicity, race, racism, privilege, ra-
cialization, stereotypes, and white supremacy. Both her understanding
of race and womanist theology then serve as the contemporary mode
of engagement with the ancient texts of Scripture in her associative
hermeneutics.

Sechrest demonstrates how her associative hermeneutics operate
when applied to particular texts that address contemporary contexts.
Sechrest's interests are the liberation of Black women and other similarly marginalized people, and she employs the tools of race studies.
This hermeneutic leads her to reject biblical texts that contain oppressive teaching. She says, "We must resist illiberative injunctions to
sustain spousal abuse (1 Pet. 3:6), injunctions that prohibit or inhibit
feminine agency (1 Cor. 14:34; 1 Tim. 2:9–15), commands to com-
mit genocide (Josh. 6–8, 10–12), or those advocating submission to
brutal governments."[50] Sechrest views associative reasoning as a skill
in which some may initially possess greater facility than others, but it
can be cultivated over time. It is the ability to draw insights from one
domain and apply them to a different environment through metaphor,
since metaphor provides a way to describe something unfamiliar by
something familiar. Sechrest acknowledges the historical and cultural
distance between her contemporary context and the Bible, so she
rejects any notion of literally reading the Bible to address modern
life. She believes the Bible can speak to contemporary ethics in cases
where "a biblical situation *is analogous* to a modern situation when
the two situations share crucial characteristics or social dynamics."[51]
Since determining the analogy is a skill that employs metaphor, Sechrest calls it "poetics," and she calls the analogy a "rhyme." She

50. Sechrest, *Race & Rhyme*, 14.
51. Sechrest, *Race & Rhyme*, 24 (emphasis original).

says, "This method presupposes an in-depth understanding of *both the historical context and the modern dilemma* to draw parallels,"[52] and so it requires creative and imaginative skill, as well as literacy and knowledge.

In her teaching experience Sechrest finds that students are more likely to succeed in creating modern "rhymes" with narrative texts than didactic texts. Not only is in-depth understanding of the ancient text and modern context important, but rigorous examinations of the biblical and modern situation are essential to determine the analogical limits between the two. For example, she says the biblical situation of Acts 6:1–6 shares enough similarities to modern times to teach an ethic of affirmative action, yet in the case of 1 Timothy 2:8–15, she finds the modern situation too dissimilar to the biblical situation for the text to be interpreted literally. Sechrest believes the text encourages women to adopt culturally appropriate behavior, but since modern concepts of such behavior differ vastly from ancient Greco-Roman norms, the text's literal injunctions are to be inverted for the current cultural moment of female empowerment. The biblical situation and modern situation must be scrutinized to determine if they possess sufficient similarities to warrant an analogy, and once the analogy is constructed it is examined under the theological rubric of whether it causes moral harm. Sechrest investigates whether the affirmative action analogy with Acts 6:1–6 can be extended to include reparations for minoritized communities, but she finds the latter is too complex to draw an analogy with the passage; thus, if one were drawn it would be morally harmful. Sechrest is quick to turn to different texts to inform the modern situation should an analogy fail with one passage. Her hermeneutic thus involves a commitment to the breadth of Scripture's manifold teachings and to reading the Bible intertextually. So when treating a topic such as race, Sechrest considers it important to examine biblical teaching on the topic across the New Testament.

---

52. Sechrest, *Race & Rhyme*, 25 (emphasis original).

Conclusion

These four scholars were chosen because each attempts to read the Bible contextually and theologically. Theology and culture mutually inform each other such that their readings of Scripture have been shaped by both their social and religious commitments. These authors were not selected for their particular theological convictions or contextual situations per se, but rather for the manner in which they integrate their cultural and spiritual concerns when reading Scripture. Readers of this volume need not imitate them unless they share the same theological and contextual concerns. Instead, readers should learn from how these four theologians respond to the religious, cultural, and pastoral questions of their day, and then attempt a similar kind of practice in their own context and with their own theological convictions. Because the gospel of Jesus Christ is infinitely translatable, the church is authorized to recontextualize it. Christian discipleship involves both preservation and innovation since "every scribe who has become a disciple in the kingdom of heaven is like the master of a household who brings out of his treasure what is new and what is old" (Matt. 13:52).

7

The Case for Theological
and Contextual Interpretation

Can Contextual Interpretation Be Theological?

If contextual interpretation is to qualify as God-talk, as I have been
arguing, then it too must be challenged. Poorly conceived contextual
interpretations, as well as poorly constructed theological interpretations, can lead to adverse consequences in the life of the church.
Charles Marsh provides a theological framework for constructing
contextual theologies through the Lived Theology Project. Marsh defines lived theology as "the foregrounding of embodied particularity
in theological narrative."[1] It elevates embodiment within theological
methodology, given Christianity's own claim that authentic faith is
verified through faithful witness rather than intellectual prowess.
Lived theology is an attempt to appropriate the narrated accounts
of faith-formed lives into the theological process. In this regard it
crosses disciplinary boundaries between theology and social theory,
ethnography, and anthropology, and it creates space within the theological task to include the contributions of life narratives, testimoni-
als, biography, and observed experiences. Resources that are typically

1. Marsh, introduction to *Lived Theology*, 7.

considered "nontheological" are the means by which the church can reclaim a doctrine of creation and reflect on its social and historical location, the two elements Willie James Jennings identifies as absent from traditional Christian theological inquiry.[2] Marsh writes, "Lived theology is therefore based on the rationale that the concrete forms of God's presence and action in the world promise rich and generative material for theological method, style, and pedagogy."[3] For lived theology, engaging embodied particularity is not a second-order activity of translation after theology has already been determined. Rather, it is enmeshed into the theological process. This methodological move creates the possibility for mutually informing interactions between the traditional disciplines of theology and the contributions from particular experiences and contexts. It is an attempt to follow Johann Bengel's dictum to "apply the text to the whole self and to apply the whole self to the text."[4]

Simon Chan also champions the notion of a lived theology when he writes, "Contextual theologies emerge as the church lives out its given script in new situations. In other words, *theology is first a lived experience of the church* before it is a set of ideas formulated by church theologians."[5] Chan provides theological justification for lived theology by citing Prosper of Aquitaine, a disciple of Augustine: *Ut legem credendi lex statuat supplicandi* (The rule of prayer should determine the rule of faith).

Lived theology is inevitably a messy process since the goal is to honor the contingencies and complexities of creation. Theological and contextual interpreters read the Bible from the perspective of a faith rooted in the Christian tradition and their cultural experience. They then use the resources necessary to study both arenas of inquiry and develop practices for their own emerging tradition. Kathryn Tanner argues that the boundaries between Christian and non-Christian ways of life are fluid and permeable. She writes, "Christian identity is therefore no longer a matter of unmixed purity, but a hybrid

---

2. Jennings, *Christian Imagination*, 4–11.
3. Marsh, introduction to *Lived Theology*, 8.
4. Bengel, *Novum Testamentum Graecum*, preface as cited in Moberly, "What Is Theological Interpretation," 168.
5. Chan, *Grassroots Asian Theology*, 15 (emphasis added).

affair established through unusual uses of materials found elsewhere. Nor can Christian identity be understood from isolated attention to Christian practices per se; understanding it now requires the careful situating of Christian practices within the wider field of cultural life on which they are a commentary."[6] By engaging their contexts, theological and contextual interpreters intentionally and explicitly reflect on their hybrid identities as Christians.

In an edited volume on the topic of Scripture, theology, and culture, Joel Green's essay outlines the three most dominant models of engagement between the ancient biblical text and the contemporary context.[7] In what he calls the "scientific frame," the historical study of the biblical text is prioritized so that little concern is given to the significance of the Bible for today. In the "contextual frame," serious attention is given to understanding the Bible's message in its ancient context and only then to exploring its relevance for modern life. Green criticizes the "scientific frame" for leaving the Bible in the past and the "contextual frame" for failing to consider all that modern readers bring to the interpretive process. He then proposes a "discursive frame" where readers acknowledge the questions and assumptions they bring to the text, and a circular dialogue is created between texts and readers. In the first model no path exists between ancient text and modern reader; the second model provides only a one-way street; and in the third model the communication travels in both directions. Theological interpretation has been forthright in acknowledging its ecclesial location and interests in this two-way engagement with the Scriptures. If Green's "discursive frame" is a model for TIS, then reading the Bible theologically for diverse ecclesial communities begins by intentionally and explicitly naming the unique cultural characteristics and interests of communities of faith. What makes these readings theological is that they are practiced by communities of faith, so various critical and cultural interpretations of the Bible are read along with the church's traditions within the context of Christian worship and ministry.

While Green and other TIS scholars affirm a discursive methodology, very few examples of its practice for diverse ecclesial communities

6. Tanner, *Theories of Culture*, 152.
7. Green, "Discursive Frame."

of faith exist. The question remains, What would it look like for underrepresented communities of faith to read the Bible theologically?
Sarah Coakley provides a model for reading the Bible for diverse communities of faith in her *God, Sexuality, and the Self*. Her theological
methods are traditional, as she thinks trinitarian doctrines emerge
"in primary interaction with Scripture, become intensified and contested in early Christian tradition, and are purified in the crucible of
prayer."[8] Like many TIS scholars who argue that theology is a spiritual practice rooted in the Christian virtues, Coakley considers ascetic
practices the precondition for doing trinitarian theology. She writes,
"Simply put, and conversely: if one is resolutely *not* engaged in the
practices of prayer, contemplation, and worship, then there are certain
sorts of philosophical insight that are unlikely, if not impossible, to
come available to one."[9] As an ascetic exercise, theology involves
the metaphysical and epistemological, personal and political, bodily
practice and intellectual engagement, and disorienting response and
transformation of one's thoughts and desires.

This theological method, which Coakley calls *théologie totale*,
"puts contemplation at its heart, but spirals out to acknowledge the
complexity of the entanglement of the secular and the spiritual realms
for those who dare to practise it,"[10] and it "insists on the sweated-out
significance of embodied (and thus gendered, and socially located)
contemplation, not mere verbal play or abstract thought."[11] This is
an embodied and lived theology. This theology is discursive in that
it involves an utter submission to God so that the desire for God su-
persedes all other human desires. However, rather than render topics
such as gender, class, or race as secondary or peripheral, it presses
into them. Coakley summarizes, "In short, *théologie totale* makes
the bold claim that the more systematic one's intentions, the more

8. Coakley, *God, Sexuality, and the Self*, 2.
9. Coakley, *God, Sexuality, and the Self*, 16 (emphasis original). It ought to be
noted that ascetic practices, often commended by practitioners of TIS as necessary
for reading the Scriptures faithfully, may not produce salutary effects. Lauren Winner narrates occasions of how the practices of the Eucharist, prayer, and baptism
themselves may be corrupted and consequently injure the lives of people and distort
doctrine. See Winner, *Dangers of Christian Practice*.
10. Coakley, *God, Sexuality, and the Self*, 59.
11. Coakley, *God, Sexuality, and the Self*, 59.

necessary the exploration of such dark and neglected corners; and that, precisely as a theology in via, *théologie totale* continually risks destabilization and redirection."[12]

If Coakley is correct, then the absence of theological interpretation for diverse communities of faith may be due to two factors: (1) the practitioners of theological interpretation lack diversity and (2) underrepresented persons have not sufficiently reflected theologically on the ways their faith is embodied. Coakley includes ethnography in her theological method to account for the ways theology is always embodied. In addition, the desire for safety and efficiency may prevent an honest engagement with culture. Coakley's *God, Sexuality, and the Self* is a trinitarian engagement of sexuality and equally an exploration of sexuality within the Trinity. She recognizes this kind of theology will destabilize and redirect, yet it is precisely the kind of reflexive, discursive, and often risky interaction between the Scriptures and contemporary life that leads to genuine transformation. This is the kind of theology that ought to characterize the interpretation of the Bible for persons on the margins.

If theological interpretation is to serve a culturally diverse church, a *théologie totale* will require the participation of an *église totale*. Given that academic biblical interpretation and theology are embedded within Western social structures, it will take more than the addition of a few diverse voices to engage in authentic, mutually informing, and transformative discourse. And given that scholars of color are tasked to master two or more kinds of academic discourse, it will take time for them to integrate contextual and traditional approaches to theology. What remains to be seen is how traditional forms of theology will respond to this cultural diversity.

Reading the Bible Figurally and Contextually

One stream of theological interpretation is figural interpretation, practiced by ancient Christian interpreters; revived in the twentieth century by Erich Auerbach, Hans Frei, and Brevard Childs; and more recently championed by North American evangelical Anglicans.

---

12. Coakley, *God, Sexuality, and the Self*, 48.

Figural interpretation is not exclusive to practitioners of TIS, but it has proved very influential for those committed to canonical readings of Scripture where literal and historical meanings continue to play an important role. In figural interpretation, the Christian canonical narrative is the primary context in which the Bible is read so that "figuration or typology [is] a natural extension of literal interpretation. It [is] literalism at the level of the whole biblical story and thus of the depiction of the whole of historical reality."[13] Auerbach describes the logic of this interpretive method:

> Figural interpretation establishes a connection between events or persons in such a way that the first signifies not only itself but also the second, while the second involves or fulfils the first. The two poles of a figure are separated in time, but both, being real events or persons, are within temporality. . . . The connection between occurrences is not regarded as primarily a chronological or causal development but as a oneness within the divine plan, of which all occurrences are parts and reflections.[14]

Reformation scholars such as Martin Luther and John Calvin, with their hermeneutics of law and gospel or promise and fulfillment, respectively, interpreted the Bible according to this tradition. Following the model of Calvin, Frei maintains the importance of the literal and historical sense of Scripture according to the canonical narrative rather than the criteria of historical criticism. He writes:

> Literal, realistic interpretation tends to set forth the sense of single stories within the Bible, naturally holding in one their explicative meaning and, where appropriate, their real reference. Figural interpretation, on the other hand, still holding together explication and reference, is a grasp of a common pattern of occurrence and meaning together, the pattern being dependent on the reality of the unitary temporal sequence which allows all the single narrations within it to become parts of a single narration.[15]

---

13. Frei, *Eclipse of Biblical Narrative*, 2.
14. Auerbach, "Figura," 53, as quoted in Frei, *Eclipse of Biblical Narrative*, 28–29.
15. Frei, *Eclipse of Biblical Narrative*, 34.

Key to figural interpretation is determining the patterns within Scripture—that is, the relationships between events, persons, and texts established by the narrative. The real world is interpreted through the lens of the biblical story, and the patterns within Scripture serve as the hermeneutic to interpret the significance of events in contemporary life.

Modern biblical criticism redefined the literal and historical in primarily lexical and scientific terms, which inevitably led to conflicts between biblical studies and the Christian tradition. A return to figural readings has been one of the motivations to recover precritical interpretation, and some proponents of TIS have defined theological interpretation in this manner. When viewed within the context of Christian tradition, historical criticism stands out as an innovation of modernity and a departure from the church's practice of theological interpretation. Frei writes, "The task of interpretation is to garner the sense of the narrative, *and not interfere with it* by uniting historical and/or narrative sequence with a logically distinct meaning that may be either the interpreter's own perspective or an amalgam of narrative event and interpretation."[16] The use of biblical criticism, even when integrated with the biblical story, is "interference" with the canonical narrative. This recovery of precritical interpretation has not led to an outright rejection of historical criticism but a chastening of it. For example, Brevard Childs, considered by many to be a model of theological and canonical interpretation and one who advocated for the recovery of precritical interpretation,[17] continued to engage source, form, and redaction criticism in his commentaries.[18] It is not really a matter of whether proponents of figural interpretation will engage in historical criticism; the question is how they will choose to do so.

Some evangelical Anglicans who practice figural interpretation have chosen to prioritize Nicene doctrine and focus on the role of Scripture in trinitarian relationships in the economy of salvation. Don Collett writes, "Stated more plainly, the Bible must speak figurally because it is a book *about* God."[19] For him, the theological purpose

16. Frei, *Eclipse of Biblical Narrative*, 36–37 (emphasis added).
17. Childs, *Struggle to Understand Isaiah*.
18. See, e.g., Childs, *Book of Exodus*; Childs, *Isaiah*.
19. Collett, *Figural Reading*, 55 (emphasis original).

of Scripture relativizes all its contents in light of its message about God. Collett claims, "Figural reading, like biblical prophecy, offers a totalizing vision of future, past, and present. Indeed, it swallows up all historical reality by enclosing all historical worlds within the scope of its theological vision."[20] A circular logic is operative in his hermeneutic since "figure is a historical reality whose original integrity and sense is rooted in a providentially constructed history, the theological significance of which is mediated in and through Scripture's literal sense."[21] The literal and historical aspects of Scripture are essential to understanding the Bible's message yet can also be properly understood only in light of the canonical narrative. Like many other proponents of TIS, Collett defines theological interpretation solely over and against historical criticism and ignores the concerns of contextual and ideological interpreters. He writes:

> Although we may learn many things about Scripture's history—including its cultural, social, and political contexts—in the end the reality it speaks of will remain a puzzle to us. . . . If we read any book, and most especially Scripture, "against the grain" in a way that is contrary to its aim, intention, or purpose (or what the fathers called its *skopos*), we will not be able to enter into its mind (*dianoia*) and come to terms with its overall unity and purpose. Reading Scripture as though it were merely a historical exercise not only fails to do justice to the theological *res* and subject matter but also ignores the purpose for which Scripture was given—namely, to serve as the inspired instrument of the triune God's self-disclosure in Christ by the Spirit.[22]

When the cultural, social, and political are spoken of only in relationship to historical criticism in which they function as unsolvable puzzles, then these aspects of Scripture as well as their contemporary correlations are considered to be outside the realm of Scripture's totalizing vision.

I have much appreciation for Collett's work and find it useful for my own thinking. But like many scholars of TIS, he overstates his case

---

20. Collett, *Figural Reading*, 55.
21. Collett, *Figural Reading*, 47.
22. Collett, *Figural Reading*, 53.

by fixating on critiquing historical criticism. If the historical sense of Scripture is an important aspect of its literal and figural sense, and history involves the social, cultural, and political, then investigation into how these concerns factor into biblical interpretation and its contemporary application ought not to be considered reading "against the grain." Creation and providence subsume human culture, societies, and politics in the past and present and thus should be considered important factors in God's economy of salvation. Scripture and the Christian tradition do make totalizing claims, so such verbiage and ideas fall within the bounds of theological discourse. While human knowledge and understanding of social, cultural, and political realities in the past and present are limited, such is the case with other theological subdisciplines like philosophy, which continues to play an important role for many theologians.

My critique of Collett concerns not so much what he claims but what he omits. Rather than narrowing the criteria for theological interpretation, I would like to expand it. The fact that Scripture is the instrument to maintain trinitarian relationships and the redemptive agent within God's economy of salvation opens up the possibility of observing social and cultural insights within the text. More importantly, this fact calls God's people to consider how the social, cultural, and political figure into God's redemptive plans. Brian Blount cites Matthew 7:21, "Not everyone who says to me 'Lord, Lord,' shall enter the kingdom of heaven," as an example "that even passages that are primarily soteriological and christological are not understood completely unless one takes into account the social dimensions that also contribute to their meanings. Inversely, one must recognize the presence of soteriological and christological features in the overtly social passages."[23] If sociology informs soteriology and Christology, and vice versa, then figural and contextual interpretations ought to be mutually informing as well.

Like Collett, Ephraim Radner uses the term "figural" to refer to the Christian tradition's reading of the Scriptures prior to the Enlightenment. He acknowledges that the phrase "figural reading" is derived from the literary trope of having one "figure" represent

---

23. Blount, *Cultural Interpretation*, 6.

another. Radner observes that by the eighteenth century a "figural reading" of Scripture was synonymous with the "spiritual" reading of the church fathers, an interpretation that was set in contrast to the modern "historical" sense. Used in this manner, the term is inclusive of either the medieval triad of allegory (matters of faith), tropology (matters of morals), and anagogy (matters of our final end), or the Protestant dyad of typology and allegory. Included in "figural" is the literal, historical, and figurative so the scope of biblical interpretation is in this manner comprehensive. Radner explains:

> "Figural," as I will try to explain in this volume, finally refers to the "everything" of God's act in creation, as it is "all" given in the Scriptures. And "figural reading" of the Bible is that reading that receives this divinely-given "allness"—who is the Christ "through whom all things and through whom we exist" (1 Cor. 8:6), who "is before all things, and in [whom] all things hold together" (Col. 1:17)—from within the breadth of the Word written.[24]

Radner acknowledges that figural reading is not an interpretive method but rather a theological affirmation and an ongoing theological task. For followers of Jesus, the scriptural story is the foundational and comprehensive narrative under which all things, the totality of existence, is to be interpreted. For example, in the case of the biblical exile Radner says, "The movement from historical *exilium* (or *captivitas*) to existential *peregrinatio* becomes not only a fluid possibility but a permanent connection: 'this world' is a world of 'exile' in which we 'make our way.'"[25] Rather than confine the theological significance of the biblical exile to its role within trinitarian relationships and a dogmatic understanding of the economy of salvation, Radner reflects on how all aspects of contemporary existence might be figured into it. He writes:

> God's purposes are presented in the experienced—temporal— becoming of human creatures into full conformity with figures of the divine text. Hence, every scriptural "exile" at every "time" is the

24. Radner, *Time and the Word*, 7.
25. Radner, *Time and the Word*, 30.

actual referent of the text itself, for all these times are in fact the times that Jesus means, given that the whole of the Scriptures in all their parts order existence in a way that Jesus has embraced as his own for the sake of and for sharing with the world. Exile and restoration are both artifacts of Scripture with which we are presented by God, and in Christ; and their "times" will proliferate variously within the experienced lives of individual creatures. In fact, the more they do so, the fuller our scriptural existences—the ultimate order of our lives—will become.[26]

For Radner figural interpretation of the Bible provides a totalizing narrative, and therefore all aspects of human existence, which presumably include the social, cultural, and political, may be ordered by the scriptural narrative. Thus, figural interpretation expands rather than limits the scope of biblical interpretation. Radner comments, "Figural readings proliferate, as Augustine suggested, for this reason: they cannot be tied down, except to the forms of God's own self, in Christ."[27] The end result of this form of figural interpretation is the multiplication of readings, not the reduction of them. Rather than running against the grain of Scripture, the social, cultural, and political provide the theological warrant to engage in contextual biblical interpretation. Given Radner's views, it is not surprising he includes a sermon by John Jasper, a former-slave-turned-preacher, titled "The Sun Do Move," among his examples of figural sermons.[28]

What does figural interpretation have to do with multicultural biblical interpretation? While the infinite translatability of Pentecost that Andrew Walls, Lamin Sanneh, and Kwame Bediako champion is a crucial Christian theological doctrine that justifies ongoing contextual interpretation of the Bible, the foundational basis of such interpretation is the prior event of Christ's fulfillment of Israel's Scriptures. One of the primary topics of interest to practitioners of TIS is the relationship between the two Testaments within the canon. As such, theological interpreters have been attentive to accusations of supersessionism and have tried to walk the tightrope of honoring

26. Radner, *Time and the Word*, 109–10.
27. Radner, *Time and the Word*, 201.
28. Radner, *Time and the Word*, 303–11.

Jewish biblical interpretation while understanding Jesus as the fulfillment of Israel's Scripture. In response to Daniel Boyarin's accusation
that Paul's reading of the Old Testament eradicates human difference and Jewish distinctiveness, John David Dawson appeals to Frei's
understanding of figural interpretation. Dawson writes, "The question of the Christian identity of persons then becomes a question of
the kind of relationship they bear in *their own* distinctive identities
to Jesus in *his own* distinctive identity."[29] Christology involves rightly
understanding Jesus's cultural identity, and if baptism initiates a person into the life of Christ, discipleship involves understanding one's
cultural identity vis-à-vis that of Christ. This debate highlights how
figural readings have everything to do with cultural and Christian
identity, as well as the fact that cultural identity is a crucial theological
issue. Theological and figural readings must attend to Jewish-gentile
relationships in Scripture, and doing so ought to sensitize readers
to ways in which various forms of human difference factor into the
biblical narrative.

Contextual theological interpretation seeks to recognize the forms
of diversity in biblical characters and how they relate to the person
of Jesus according to the Jewish-gentile logic of the canonical narrative. These understandings of Scripture impact the lives of contemporary readers as they use patterns established in the canon to
apply Scripture's teachings to events in their own day. When readers
observe that a vast array of cultures is integral to the biblical narrative
they begin to identify patterns of God's redemptive activity within
diverse contexts. These patterns serve as a hermeneutic to interpret
and apply the Scriptures to the diverse contexts in which people find
themselves. Contextual theological interpretation maintains the theological difference between, and the significance of, Jewish-gentile
relationships in Scripture and contemporary theology. Therefore, to
read biblical texts contextually in a supersessionist manner violates
the theological principle of understanding Jesus as the fulfillment
of Israel's Scripture. One need only look to the German church's
Aryan national reading of the Bible in the twentieth century to see
the dangers of "contextual" supersessionist readings.

---

29. Dawson, *Christian Figural Reading*, 176–77 (emphasis original).

Love Sechrest, whose model of associative reasoning was introduced in the previous chapter, provides a model for identifying analogical relationships between contemporary social contexts and biblical texts. She demystifies contextual readings for the skeptical and suspicious by offering a clear description of the interpretive moves involved in reading the Bible for multicultural contexts. While Sechrest's focus on womanist and liberationist theological commitments differs from the emphasis placed on trinitarian and evangelical theology espoused above, her hermeneutical model bears great similarity to that of theological interpretation.[30] The analogical thinking she describes in associative reasoning is precisely the kind of interpretive practice involved in figural interpretation, and therefore her model can be used for theological and contextual interpretation. Sechrest acknowledges that associative reasoning is a work of the imagination, where the meaning of words is transferred to a different idea in an innovative act. This form of interpretation is more art than science, and so she describes it as "poetics" and as "rhyme."

Analogies to Scripture of all sorts and stripes can be imagined ad infinitum, so more than similarities and dissimilarities between modern situations and the biblical text are required for Christian theological and contextual interpretation. Once Sechrest draws the analogy between the biblical text and modern situation, she inserts an additional interpretive step by asking whether the analogy poses moral harm. Here she acknowledges the limits of associative reasoning. The Bible and modern culture alone are not sufficient resources to produce salutary interpretations. At this point her womanist and liberationist theological commitments screen interpretations to determine whether the analogies ought to be employed. It is noteworthy that her theological commitments influence the kind of analogies she investigates, but they do not determine her interpretations from the outset. Instead, they help eliminate interpretations that do not fulfill

30. Sechrest expresses her own indebtedness to Richard Hays's analogical method in Hays, *Moral Vision*, and she describes how her work differs from his by centering womanist liberation in place of Hays's focus on cross, community, and new creation. Sechrest, *Race & Rhyme*, 3n5. K. K. Yeo, whose work was also highlighted in the previous chapter, also cites Hays's work, this time on typology, to support a cross-cultural hermeneutic. Yeo, *Rhetorical Interaction*, 212–13.

her purposes for reading the Bible. One might call this interpretive step reading the Bible according to a rule of faith. Theological interpreters have been forthright about reading the Bible according to the rule of faith and have been criticized for overdetermined biblical interpretation. Certainly some are guilty as charged.[31]

In my mind a rule of faith should not factor so much at the beginning, but rather late in the interpretive process in the way Sechrest does so as not to "rule" or determine interpretations but to *rule out* interpretations that do not align with theological commitments. Given my contextual concerns, trinitarian theology and the gospel do not dominate and predetermine how I read biblical texts, but several questions do play an important role: How does this interpretation figure into the life, death, and resurrection of Jesus? Does this reading align with a trinitarian understanding of God? Persons who read Scripture both contextually and theologically will interpret individual texts in relationship to sociocultural aspects of contemporary life as well as in congruence with the understanding of God revealed in Jesus Christ. The Bible's story includes important social contexts, so historical criticism can play an important role in understanding particular texts. However, this form of interpretation eschews historical reconstructions that run counter to an understanding of Scripture that finds its fulfillment in the life, death, and resurrection of Christ. The Bible presents diverse portrayals of God and sanctions lament and theodicy, yet it understands these as descriptions and means of worshiping the Father, Son, and Holy Spirit. Ideological interpretations that insist that texts present a different portrait of God for *every* reader ought to be rejected. I acknowledged earlier (chap. 3) that some biblical texts may challenge a traditional trinitarian understanding of God, but it is another thing to assert that they always will do so. For this very reason theological interpretation must be *contextual*, and interpreters must exercise great wisdom and discernment.

Reading the Bible as described above is both a more expansive and reductive reading of Scripture. If the scope of Scripture's witness is all of creation and redemption, then God's people ought to pursue how

---

31. Many of the Brazos Theological Commentaries have been criticized for this reason.

Scripture testifies to all aspects of creaturely existence. The belief that no topic under the sun is beyond the bounds of Scripture provides theological warrant to pursue all forms of contextual interpretation. At the same time, the belief that Scripture's primary role is to reveal God and testify to God's plan of redemption ought to chasten human expectations for the Bible. People have repeatedly said that the Bible is not primarily a history textbook or science textbook, but humans have made a legion of claims on every topic under the sun supposedly based on the authority of the Bible. Much of liberationist and postcolonial interpretation's task is to identify these abuses of Scripture and demonstrate the ways in which the Bible can be used as an instrument of harm or present a view of God contrary to that of the Christian belief. Particularly because of the Bible's immense scope and diversity of materials, it can be interpreted to support an infinite number of claims. Readers may expect too much from the Bible, whether it be dietary instructions or gender norms for contemporary life. Social conservatives often assume the Bible provides clear teaching on such matters and assert their normativity. In response, critics assert that the Bible ought to be rejected for precisely these reasons. Theological interpretation assumes that the Bible provides a witness to the totality of existence but does not provide definitive teaching on all matters. Scripture is sufficient for life, but it is not exhaustive.

The Limits of Contextual Interpretation

While understanding one's context is an essential aspect of reading the Bible faithfully, there are limitations in doing so. Cultures are complex, diverse, and constantly evolving, and the analyses of cultures are often highly contested and politicized. People differ over the validity of various instruments and methods used to analyze and interpret cultures. Conservatives and progressives may claim some methodologies are tainted by ideological biases, and they may consider some to be heterodox. In a time of intense culture wars over sexuality, gender, race, and nationality, interpreting context is fraught with differing viewpoints and debate. The way forward is not to dismiss contextual study or attempt to canonize a particular method, but rather to engage in honest, rigorous, and open interdisciplinary study. This form of research is done best by those conversant in multiple disciplines who appreciate and critique the contributions of each.

Jonathan Tran's work *Asian Americans and the Spirit of Racial Capitalism* provides an example of both the contributions and limitations of contextual study. The topics of his book are race and racism, but the lessons learned from his work can apply to the study of other aspects of culture. In order to write a constructive and critical work of both theology and race, he claims, "I must insist that the conceptual work necessary for my argument requires speaking both languages and inhabiting both worlds."[32] He thus defines his contextual and theological method:

1. Empirical facts *qua* facts speak for themselves.
2. Given enough time and pushed far enough, empirical facts admit of—analytically and synthetically (logically and experientially), using the old distinction—theological facts (i.e., facts about the world reveal facts about God).
3. Therefore, while theology sits in the background of valid arguments about race, it need sometimes come to the fore.[33]

Tran rigorously applies this method to examine identarian antiracism, which portrays racism as the personal and systemic denigration of certain races by other races, most often in the form of harm committed by white people toward Black people. He notes that identarian antiracists look past some of the empirical facts regarding metaphysical questions and "adopt the notion of race not because they have worked it out, but because their politics requires it."[34] That is, their commitment to antiracism against white supremacy determines their understanding of race so that "identarian antiracism racializes."[35] In regard to Asian American racism, Tran demonstrates that many academic efforts to combat the model minority myth actually assume the myth's logics and therefore reinscribe its basic narrative. Tran devotes much of his work to arguing that white supremacy ought

32. Tran, *Asian Americans*, xxi.
33. Tran, *Asian Americans*, xxi.
34. Tran, *Asian Americans*, 3.
35. Tran, *Asian Americans*, 3.

not to be mythologized as a metaphysical claim, but that it ought to be exposed as a hierarchical system of domination created for capitalistic exploitation. He finds "the lack of historical attention sends antiracism off the rails. Antiracists have lent whiteness greater power than it would have on its own."[36]

Tran's concerns are not merely academic, and his analysis of race and racism is not merely based on the social sciences; it also includes theology. His primary thesis is "that Marxism, like Christianity, calls for collective revolutionary action but, given its ambivalence about ethical life, and religion in particular, often lacks the determinate forms of life necessary to get revolution off the ground."[37] Tran employs social scientific tools to understand racism, but he recognizes their limitations in offering a solution to it. He argues that shifting the focus away from racial identity to political economy will more effectively lead to liberation, and here he proposes that the solution to combat racism is to pursue what he calls a "deep economy," or what Christians call "the divine economy" that consists of the following:

1. In the ecology of God's creation, everything is connected.
2. The substance of these connections, and therefore running through everything, is God's love.
3. Under the conditions of sin, God's love takes the reparative form of justice and mercy.
4. Creatures participate in and reveal God's reparative justice and mercy through processes and commitments of liberation.
5. Liberation, by which creatures participate in and reveal God, is the most natural thing in the world.[38]

In this view, "the primary political key of Christian witness is not resistance but proclamation,"[39] and since racism's fundamental motivations are economic, Tran argues that the primary means of defeating racism is to construct new economic ecologies according to the values of the divine economy.

36. Tran, *Asian Americans*, 135.
37. Tran, *Asian Americans*, 293.
38. Tran, *Asian Americans*, 207.
39. Tran, *Asian Americans*, 207.

Tran's study provides an example of the importance of both employing and critiquing contextual and theological resources. Since Christians adopted racist logics within their theologies for the sake of maintaining exploitative economies, Tran finds Marxist tools important for their ability to expose systemic inequities. Yet he also acknowledges their limitations in addressing metaphysical questions and providing spiritual and ethical models. As noted in an earlier chapter, R. S. Sugirtharajah demonstrates that postcolonial biblical criticism offers nothing constructive and exists solely to decenter hegemonic forces. In North America, where so much of public life is racialized, including academic biblical interpretation, contextual biblical interpreters would do well to clarify the methodologies and aims of race-based forms of biblical interpretation. It is not uncommon for biblical interpreters to adopt popular tropes in their contextual analysis, such as "whiteness" or "model minority." By their use, are biblical interpreters reinscribing racist logics and making metaphysical claims? Is raced-based biblical interpretation just another form of identarian politics? Should all race-based forms of biblical interpretation (Black, Latino/a, Asian American interpretations) be antiracist? Tran's study demonstrates the importance of critically analyzing modes of cultural analysis to see if they accurately reflect empirical facts and whether they rest on metaphysical assumptions that align with Christian beliefs.

The Limits of Christian Tradition

Even though I have argued that Christian doctrine and tradition ought to play an important hermeneutical role in biblical interpretation, their limitations also need to be acknowledged. Christian tradition was never a fixed reality. It is marked with diversity and division, and it continues to evolve. Tradition may serve epistemological, existential, and communal needs, but its contribution to these purposes ought to be considered of relative value. Turning to tradition for epistemological certainty ends only in idolatry. Seeking existential comfort in tradition can result in ecclesiastical fetishism, and while tradition may unite Christian communities, it can also contribute to their insularity. Theological interpreters may look to Nicene Christianity or to

Christianity's first millennium for a rule of faith,[40] as long as these are heuristic rather than absolute models. John Webster offers the sober reminder that "there is no pure Christian past whose retrieval can ensure theological fidelity,"[41] as well as personal and communal security and happiness. While calls to either wholly embrace or reject tradition are quite common, tradition's contribution is best realized when it is appreciated for its relative value rather than in all-or-nothing terms.

How then does one use a resource of relative value? Eastern Orthodox theologian David Bentley Hart attempts to identify the limitations of tradition as well as its positive contributions to the Christian faith in his book, *Tradition and Apocalypse*. Hart is well aware that history demonstrates that tradition is more often marked by chaos and accidents than by order and purpose, and that formulations of Christian doctrine were often determined by forces extrinsic to Christian belief. An honest examination of the historical record reveals that tradition "had to struggle mightily to impose a consensus that had never hitherto existed, to dissolve disagreements that had persisted undetected across many generations of believers, and then to alter the record to give the impression that the terms of the armistice thus achieved were no more than the purest possible expression of something boldly confessed *ubique, semper, et ab omnibus* (to borrow the brash phrase of Vincent of Lérins): 'everywhere, always, and by all.'"[42] While apologists for tradition often look to history as their friend, history does not reciprocate this sentiment. For this reason, Hart has no patience for the religious conservatism of traditionalism, which he considers a "naïve, historically illiterate fidelity to a mythic prehistory"[43] and "infantile longing for the feeling of security."[44] Hart sharply critiques two of tradition's most influential apologists, John Henry Newman and Maurice Blondel, for claiming that tradition is "the dynamic and progressive of an ever wider and deeper and more

40. E.g., Seitz, *Nicene Christianity*; Abraham, Vickers, and Van Kirk, *Canonical Theism*.
41. Webster, "Theologies of Retrieval," 596.
42. Hart, *Tradition and Apocalypse*, 13–14.
43. Hart, *Tradition and Apocalypse*, 15.
44. Hart, *Tradition and Apocalypse*, 16.

inexhaustible reservoir of truth."[45] Hart demonstrates that Newman and Blondel ultimately make tautologous arguments that cannot
be substantiated by the historical record and that are intellectually
unsatisfactory.

The subtitle of Hart's book, *An Essay on the Future of Christian
Belief*, is noteworthy since tradition is typically viewed as an orienta-
tion toward the past, not the future. Hart asserts that eschatology
ought to be decisive in providing a theological justification for tradition. He writes, "Only by seeing the end of tradition's course—
something of its final cause—can one see its unity as a formal truth
rather than a mere confluence of material and mechanically efficient
forces."[46] Such an understanding of tradition more honestly accounts
for the formulations of doctrines in the past and clarifies the theological task in the present moment. Hart observes that Arius was a
conservative theologian in his day, that the victors at Nicaea were not
more faithful to the past, and that the result of the council cannot
be considered anything other than an innovation. Fidelity to tradition is not to be measured by whether doctrines align to the past but
instead to God's future. Thus, "Every doctrinal decision is a decision
towards a future never yet wholly disclosed,"[47] and "a tradition, in its
full theological sense, is truly vital to the degree that it is always, in
every epoch, in a state of patient but dynamic reconstruction, new
expressions of the faith and new understandings of old expressions
constantly refashioning and enlarging and altering the tradition's
own understanding of the meaning of received dogmas."[48]

Hart observes that the nature of the gospel is apocalyptic and the
kingdom of God is a disruption into the lives of humans. For centuries
Christianity flourished without officially defined dogma or a univer-
sally recognized canon of Scripture, where faithfulness was measured
according to apocalyptic expectation rather than doctrinal purity.
From this perspective, doctrine is "a language of disenchantment, a
probationary discourse that tries at once both to recuperate the force
of a cosmic disruption in the form of institutional formulae and to

45. Hart, *Tradition and Apocalypse*, 14.
46. Hart, *Tradition and Apocalypse*, 53–54.
47. Hart, *Tradition and Apocalypse*, 64.
48. Hart, *Tradition and Apocalypse*, 65.

create a stable center within history from which it might be tolerable to await a Kingdom that has been indefinitely deferred."[49] If the gospel is an apocalypse, then disruption is vital to the theological task. Hart writes, "The hermeneutical labor needed to understand any tradition requires disruption no less than stability, 'progressive' ambition no less than 'conservative' prudence, because it is only through the play of tension and resolution, stability and disintegration, that that which is most imperishable in a tradition can be fitfully perceived, or at least sensed."[50] Hart meditates on the nature of tradition in light of 1 Corinthians 13:13, "And now faith, hope, and love remain, these three, and the greatest of these is love," and concludes, "Faith is the will to let the past be reborn in the present as more than what until now had been known, and the will to let the present be shaped by a future yet to be revealed. Hope is the conviction that that revelation will not only fulfill but far exceed the promise that the tradition preserves within itself. And, in the end, faith and hope will both pass away, or rather pass over into perfect love."[51] Tradition serves a provisional role in the economy of salvation, similar to how "the law was our disciplinarian until Christ came" (Gal. 3:24).

This definition of tradition possesses the potential to radically alter theological methodologies and ecclesial processes. When appeals to tradition equate to alignment or adherence to the concrete realities of persons, councils, schools, or epochs, tradition has devolved into traditionalism. Christianity at its core is a faith in the invisible, since the visible is but an adumbration to the reality of faith, so to fixate on the visible past is to corrupt the nature of faith. Orthodoxy is then not merely to be measured on a doctrine's congruence with claims of faith in the past but whether truth claims align with the future of God. Since the gospel is an apocalypse, those committed to the gospel are to humbly and discerningly be attentive to disruptions that may result in the church refashioning and reformulating its beliefs and practices. Although conservatives may seek change in attempts to return to a mythic past and progressives may seek change in cultural

---

49. Hart, *Tradition and Apocalypse*, 77.
50. Hart, *Tradition and Apocalypse*, 79–80.
51. Hart, *Tradition and Apocalypse*, 188.

accommodations to contemporary concerns, Christian eschatology ought to be the motivator and model for the theological task.

Contextual biblical interpreters and theologians concerned about orthodoxy have largely looked to the past to justify their work. They have tried to demonstrate that their interpretations and theology are not innovations but are congruent with the Christian tradition. The church fathers are most often studied and referenced because they represent the earliest traditions and greatest potential for ecumenical engagement. Bediako represents one of many contextual theologians who feel compelled to find theological warrant in patristic writings.[52] Certainly these forms of studies are important and valuable, but if Hart's thesis is correct, they need not be the only means of demonstrating fidelity to the Christian tradition. New forms of contextual interpretation can be faithful to the Christian tradition through alignment with the eschatological goals of Christianity. As disruptions to current expressions of faith, they need not be viewed as potential distractions and detractions. Instead they can be seen as potential catalysts to refashion, expand, and reform Christian understandings of their received doctrines. K. K. Yeo finds that the doctrine of eschatology provides warrant for global hermeneutics and offers a reminder of theology's limitations: "Therefore, the Christ event, which discloses the eschatological dawning of God's truth also signals the open-endedness of truth and the limitations of our present knowledge. This eschatological reservation and call invites us into a dialogical process between cultures, a dialogue in which we can both accept but also transcend the limits of our specific cultural locations."[53] Yeo believes global hermeneutics serves the interests of all Christians since it may help address and overcome blind spots and prejudices. Thus, theological innovation may not automatically be deemed heterodox since innovation has been part of the tradition itself.

Those who value past traditions do not need to view this mode of theological inquiry as a threat. It may even help address some of the challenges facing theologies of retrieval. The history of the church

---

52. Bediako, *Theology and Identity.*
53. Yeo, "Culture and Intersubjectivity," 99.

is marked by embarrassing scandals and moral failures. Many of tradition's key figures and institutions are guilty of anti-Semitism, sexism, homophobia, imperialism and colonialism, racism, slavery, and other sins that contemporary people would find unacceptable. Many have argued the contributions of these persons and institutions ought to be rejected wholesale, which then jeopardizes the theological role of tradition. I am certainly not dismissing the severity of these sins and promoting pardon on past offenders. Quite the opposite, I believe people can be more receptive to an honest assessment of both the contributions and failures of figures in the past when they no longer view them in mythic terms. Tradition can best serve as a resource for theology and ministry when its limitations are understood.

The Text and Exegesis Still Matter

I imagine that some readers may think my emphasis on context and theology precludes a value for close readings of Scripture. Some may conclude that I do not believe the biblical text might challenge and reform our cultural and theological biases. This book is not intended to provide a comprehensive interpretive and theological method. It aims to address what I perceive as a current lacuna in current scholarship and theological education. It assumes the value and importance of biblical studies, and rather than trying to replace current exegetical methodologies, it offers a corrective on their role within theological education. The limits of context and tradition within the Christian faith are based on the premise that the Christian faith is *semper reformanda* due to the Bible's ability to challenge all theologies and cultural ideologies. This reformation principle assumes that the text and exegesis still matter and their importance ought not to be minimized.

Early African American biblical interpretation provides a compelling example for the need to read the Bible carefully in order to challenge hypocritical and oppressive ecclesial traditions and apply the Bible's teachings to the contextual needs of its readers. Emerson B. Powery and Rodney Steven Sadler say, "For African American interpreters, the meaning of slavery, fused with the worth of dark-skinned

Christian identity, demanded a critical, black hermeneutic."[54] As many have noted, theirs was a hermeneutic of survival since the Bible in the hands of the "master's minister" was the very means by which white slave owners justified slavery. Lisa Bowens notes that the Princeton theologian Charles Hodge incorrectly believed that "if slaves obey their owners and slaveholders treat them well, such actions will eventually lead to the dissolution of the practice."[55] She concludes, "Being a slave owner, therefore, did not prevent one from being a good Baptist, a good Methodist, or a good Presbyterian."[56] While certainly many Blacks despised the Bible and rejected the religion it represented, what is remarkable is that not only did many slaves willingly embrace Christianity, but the Bible became one of the most powerful tools in their liberation from slavery. It was because they carefully read the Bible to address their own sociocultural concerns that they were able to refute the false doctrines of the church of their day. Frederick Douglass's slave master noted of him, "If this one should ever be taught to read the bible, there would be no keeping him a slave,"[57] which purportedly only inspired Douglass to learn to read all the more. Douglass is arguably the most prolific critic of the use of the Bible in his day, yet even he "was not willing to hand over the Bible to the proslavery side, despite challenges Scripture itself created"[58] because he recognized its important role in the cause of abolition.

Without formal theological training or catechesis and faced with faulty interpretations of Scripture intended to dehumanize and oppress, early African American interpreters effectively championed the cause of abolition through reading the Bible, and they also embraced the God it reveals. Theirs was an innovative and creative contextual and spiritual reading of the Bible that developed at the grassroots level. Powery and Sadler summarize this hermeneutical tradition in their description of how early African Americans used the Bible:

54. Powery and Sadler, *Genesis of Liberation*, 163.
55. Bowens, *African American Readings*, 175.
56. Bowens, *African American Readings*, 175.
57. Holland, *Frederick Douglass*, 15, as cited in Powery and Sadler, *Genesis of Liberation*, 12.
58. Powery and Sadler, *Genesis of Liberation*, 131.

1. The Bible gave them hope that God would act without human (political) intervention to provide justice for enslaved Africans.

2. It grounded subversive arguments against the type of Christianity practiced by Southern slaveholders.

3. It provided a mythic system that could explain their plight and a symbolic world that resonated with their own, while demonstrating God's fidelity to those similarly situated (slaves, exiles, sufferers).

4. It allowed them the latitude to emphasize or exclude portions of Scripture based on the needs, without compromising the core of the Christian message.

5. It envisioned human origins in a manner that allowed them to discern a glorious past for African peoples and positive dimensions of African identity.[59]

Powery and Sadler say these early African Americans "employed biblical criticism, not in the sense of the 'historical criticism,' but the sense of discerning the implications of the text for ordinary people."[60] This was a biblical criticism that, as John Barton argues, is aimed at understanding the "plain meaning of the biblical text."[61] This was an exegesis that sought "*a credible and coherent understanding of the text on its own terms and in its own context.*"[62] Since these interpreters possessed little formal education, literacy and logic were sufficient to effectively practice this form of exegesis and biblical criticism. Through close readings of the Bible, early African American interpreters refuted teachings that claimed Ham/Canaan's curse (Gen. 9:22–25) justified the enslavement of Blacks, challenged the hypocrisy of white Sabbath practices, highlighted Scripture's emphasis on human equality (e.g., Acts 17:26), and even offered the countermyth that whiteness represented sin in the form of leprosy (2 Kings 5:1–27).[63]

---

59. Powery and Sadler, *Genesis of Liberation*, 3.
60. Powery and Sadler, *Genesis of Liberation*, x.
61. Barton, *Nature of Biblical Criticism*, 3.
62. Gorman, *Elements of Biblical Exegesis*, 5 (emphasis original).
63. Powery and Sadler, *Genesis of Liberation*, 63–111.

This interpretive method viewed the Bible as a sacred and life-affirming text from which African Americans received salvation and deepened a personal relationship with God. Certainly one's own experience was a vital aspect of their hermeneutic but equally so was the plain sense of Scripture. Thus, while they opposed some of the teaching and texts weaponized by their white slave owners, they did not discard the entirety of the Christian tradition and Scriptures. In her treatment of early African American readings of Paul, Bowens observes how "they shaped the Christian tradition to fit their own situation of enslavement. They engaged in a 'dual process,' accepting the gospel and at the same time making the gospel their own."[64] They "shaped," not "rejected" the Christian tradition, including even the writings of Paul, which were notoriously used for sanctioning the practice of slavery. Bowens describes the hermeneutics of early African Americans:

> An overwhelming number of the interpreters discussed in this volume employed Paul in a hermeneutic of trust; that is, these interpreters saw Scripture as God's sacred word and believed that it mattered for them, for their communities, and for the nation. Interestingly, they applied a hermeneutic of suspicion to the white interpreters of the text, such as the slaveholders, proponents of slavery, and advocates of segregation, and not to the text itself. . . . Since many black hermeneuts believed God authored the biblical text, they saw the text as life giving and affirming of their value, worth, and dignity. Correspondingly, they believed that Paul's voice spoke to their current context because for them Scripture was a living and breathing document with relevance for their lives.[65]

Rather than rejecting the Bible, these interpreters challenged what they considered faulty interpretations of the Bible. A common method of refuting slave teachings was to appeal to different texts that affirmed Black humanity and dignity. Bowens says they insisted that Scripture needed to be read in conversation with other Scripture, and they employed a canonical method when reading the Bible.

---

64. Bowens, *African American Readings*, 266.
65. Bowens, *African American Readings*, 297–98.

Early African American biblical interpretation demonstrates that communities can challenge false doctrines and oppressive interpretations of the Bible *and* embrace the Christian message of salvation and the authority of the Scriptures. Bowens describes the hermeneutics of the renowned Black female preacher Zilpha Elaw (ca. 1790–1873): "When interpreting Scripture, she understands that historical context matters as well as other scriptural witnesses, including Paul himself, and that if one evaluates the historical situation of the apostle's words, then one recognizes the temporal and situational mandate of Paul's statement and realizes that his words regarding women's silence do not function as an eternal mandate for all churches and for all time."[66] Elaw employed conventional techniques of biblical criticism and exegesis, such as reading the Bible in its historical context and reading the Bible canonically. One might argue that she and other early African American interpreters read the Bible both contextually and theologically. This form of biblical interpretation did not devalue the importance of the text and exegesis. Rather, texts and their interpretation were held alongside other important aspects of the theological task.

A recent example of a similar form of biblical interpretation is found in Elizabeth Mburu's *African Hermeneutics*. She describes African biblical hermeneutics as analogous to a four-legged stool in which parallel to the African context, the theological context, the literary context, and the historical-cultural context each serve as a leg, and the seat is application. Mburu emphasizes that each of these hermeneutical steps is necessary to the process of balanced interpretation in the same way a stool missing a leg would not achieve balance. It is worth noting that three out of Mburu's four hermeneutical steps (theological, literary, and historical-cultural contexts) are conventional practices of biblical and theological interpretation. She recognizes the interrelatedness of these steps and notes the African context is the most important of the four "legs" since the entire process of interpretation is aimed for the African context. Thus, contextual biblical interpretation does not displace exegesis and theology but incorporates and orients them for particular ends.

66. Bowens, *African American Readings*, 111.

Contextual Theological Interpretation Is a Risky but Necessary Affair

Sugirtharajah demonstrates that even texts that have been elevated as the quintessential teachings on nonviolence, such as the Sermon on the Mount, can be used to oppress others. For example, in India until M. N. Roy and Mahatma Gandhi's transgressive nonviolent interpretations, colonists used the Sermon on the Mount to silence "native" critique.[67] The converse can also be true, that texts that contain violence can be interpreted in a nonviolent manner. Biblical critics have argued that certain biblical texts that are inherently violent and even texts that are not apparently so can be interpreted in ways that oppress others, and therefore they ought to be rejected. If even the Sermon on the Mount can be read in a manner that oppresses others, any and every biblical text can be read to promote violence. The questions are: At what point should other hermeneutics buffer a hermeneutic of suspicion? What is the threshold at which a biblical text ought to be "cancelled"? At what point should biblical books be banned?

Rather than disqualify biblical texts because they carry the potential to oppress others, I suggest that communities adopt a risk-management approach in discerning how to read texts that carry the potential to cause harm. This is a community-oriented approach such that sweeping pronouncements made by academics, with no connection to these communities, that certain texts should be rejected ought to be ignored. Certainly scholars ought to warn of the potential for harmful readings, and any current use of biblical texts to abuse others ought to be challenged, but to claim that all communities ought to abandon the religious texts they consider sacred is a colonizing act.

Communication is always a risky affair. Comedians constantly straddle the fine line between entertainment and offense. Professionals know that emails are among the most volatile forms of communication where people can be misunderstood. Tweeting is even worse, yet despite their deficiencies, both email and social media are important tools of communication. Interpreting the Bible is also risky business, especially when done with the assumption that it is a sacred text. Misreadings and abuses will occur, so the question is not whether the Bible can be read to oppress others. That answer

67. Sugirtharajah, *Troublesome Texts*, 43.

is patently obvious. The question is how the Bible can be read to minimize harm, which may or may not include avoiding certain texts because of their negative associations by various persons. Risks of harmful interpretations are worth taking when communities benefit from life-giving experiences of reading Scripture. For example, the manifold ways in which the exodus story can be interpreted in illiberative ways has been well documented,[68] yet Walter Brueggemann notes that the "most convincing warrant" for a liberationist reading "is the undeniable fact that [the Exodus story] is so used, that its adherents find it to 'work.'"[69]

When someone experiences little to no benefit from Scripture, then certainly the risk of abusive Bible readings is never worth it. Whether texts that have historically been weaponized against certain communities ought to be redeemed and reread is an act of pastoral and communal discernment. Jews and Christians throughout the ages have not held every book in the Bible in the same regard, so Scriptures that have been used to harm certain communities ought not to be forced on them. What I am suggesting has been practiced among ecclesial bodies for centuries and is by no means innovative. It seems the modern obsession for hermeneutical certainty motivates ethical purity tests on texts and leads to pronouncements to decanonize biblical texts. Or it is the current state of identarian advocacy that motivates some to declare decanonized texts that have harmed their community, no matter if other communities may benefit from the same text. I acknowledge that my commitments are to a global ecclesial community, so communal discernment is a complex task, and unity is elusive since it requires negotiating between diverse experiences with the Scriptures.

As I have been arguing, I would like to see strict disciplinary divisions set aside in favor of contextual and theological interpretation for the sake of Christian ministry in multicultural contexts. One school of thought that has explicitly claimed a *théologie totale* is classic liberation theology. As discussed in a previous chapter, classic liberation theologians attempted to resist the dualities of sacred/secular and

68. Collins, *Bible After Babel*, 57–60.
69. Brueggemann, "Pharoah as Vassal," 27, as quoted in Collins, *Bible After Babel*, 60.

individual/communal. Typically they have been categorized within the discipline of "contextual interpretation" and not "theological interpretation." Because of these labels, theological interpreters have overlooked the theological contribution of contextual interpreters. Ironically it is the postcolonial critic Sugirtharajah who considers classic liberation interpreters too "theological" when he evaluates Gustavo Gutiérrez's reading of Job and Elsa Tamez's reading of Paul.[70] He writes, "For both, the credibility of the Bible is defined by and based on *its essential content—Jesus Christ.*"[71] He concludes his critique by saying, "Their hermeneutical proposal sounds as though it is replicating the liberal message, couched in liberation language: Jesus loves me. This I know for the Bible tells me so."[72] Sugirtharajah recognizes that this is not fundamentalism or grassroots contextual theology; in this case, "the Book of Job and the Pauline writings are reread, not using any specific Latin American theological nuances, or indigenous cultural resources, but from the perspective of liberal and modernist values of solidarity, identification, and liberation."[73]

Sugirtharajah rightly observes that Gutiérrez and Tamez have employed theological language in their appropriation of modern values. Some theological interpreters may reject their interpretations on the basis of their appropriation of modern concepts, perhaps pointing to the failures of Protestant liberal theology in the twentieth century to support their argument. It is beyond the scope of this work to provide a thorough critique of Protestant liberal theology. I simply say that I do not believe theologies ought to be dismissed simply because they appropriate Western modern concepts like solidarity, any more than I think a Korean Christian theology ought to be dismissed for its appropriation of a Korean concept such as *han*. In both cases, it needs to be asked whether the appropriation of these cultural concepts is congruent with the message of the gospel or replaces it. As Sanneh has demonstrated, Christian theology has always been translated into different languages and cultures. All Christian theologies, both conservative and liberal, Western and non-Western, are susceptible

---

70. Gutiérrez, *On Job*; Tamez, *Amnesty of Grace*.
71. Sugirtharajah, *Postcolonial Criticism*, 112 (emphasis added).
72. Sugirtharajah, *Postcolonial Criticism*, 112.
73. Sugirtharajah, *Postcolonial Criticism*, 112.

to the idolatries of cultural accommodation and political power. My point is that if the commentaries by Gutiérrez and Tamez adhere to the criteria of theological interpretation, they ought to be included within the readings, perhaps even within the canon, for contextual interpretation as well as theological interpretation.

The cultural and theological interchange that I propose involves risk. The church and academy share an anxiety over the fragmentation of biblical interpretation should the various contexts or communities of interpretation become too numerous or narrowly defined. While diversity is valued in Christianity, too much of it threatens the church's catholicity. Identarian politics are operative not only in the academy and elsewhere in society but also in ecclesial bodies. An overemphasis on cultural difference can threaten the unity of the church and lead to sectarianism. Thus, how one responds to the diversity within the church and how Christians are to engage diversity in the culture are some of the most pressing theological tasks facing the church today. Cultural diversity and catholicity have been theological and pastoral issues from the church's inception, so engaging diverse biblical interpretation ought not to be perceived as something peripheral or avant-garde for theologians. If the cacophony of Pentecost did not deter the apostles from ministering to people from every nation, theologians today who confess to believe in one, holy, catholic, and apostolic church ought to follow suit. In the twentieth and twenty-first centuries, the church and societies have experienced change, diversity, and disruption at a scale and pace never seen before. Christian ministry requires humility, wisdom, courage, and imagination to discern theological faithfulness to the gospel. Biblical interpretation has no other option but to be theological and contextual to accomplish this goal. My prayer is that this book is helpful for Christian ministers and those who educate them to do just that.

Appendix

A Proposed Pedagogy for Theological and Contextual Interpretation

In many curricula, and in evangelical settings particularly, students take biblical courses first, and often biblical studies serves as the foundation for studying the other theological disciplines. In these Bible courses students learn an interpretive methodology then apply biblical insights gained from this hermeneutic to their study of other theological disciplines. In such a curriculum, students may never reexamine or modify the hermeneutic learned in their initial Bible courses in light of the theological contributions of their church history, theology, and practical ministry courses. They may assume that the Bible is to be applied to the other disciplines in a unidirectional manner and never inquire how their understanding of the Bible is to be shaped by the rest of the curriculum.

In this book I have argued that theological and contextual interpretation is an advanced activity where biblical exegesis, church history,

An early form of this proposal was presented as "Diversifying Syllabi for the Sake of Theological and Contextual Interpretation," History of Biblical Interpretation Research Group, Institute of Biblical Research, San Antonio, TX, November 17, 2023.

theology, and practical ministry courses are prerequisites. Contextual and theological interpretation defies the methodological categories within biblical studies, leading interpreters far beyond the traditional boundaries of the discipline. I do not believe the solution is to move biblical studies courses to the end of the curriculum. Reading primary sources, gaining exegetical skills, and developing facility with the Old and New Testaments remain foundational and serve contextual and theological biblical interpretation, so they ought to be learned early in one's studies.

My course on reading the Old Testament theologically and contextually is an upper division elective for students who have already been introduced to the Old and New Testaments, have been taught and practiced exegesis, and have taken several courses in theology, church history, and practical theology. The students who have benefited most from the course are those who have a good grasp of their theological commitments, are able to do exegesis, have reflected on their sociocultural identity, and possess a good understanding of their ministry context. My course draws from various theological disciplines and invites students into both a constructive and a deconstructive exercise. In my experience, the course serves students best as a capstone to their education.

Yet I do not believe theological and contextual biblical interpretation should be reserved for a capstone course; it ought to be scaffolded into a curriculum. At my seminary, theological and biblical interpretation is introduced from day one, and students get exposure to it throughout their studies. The result, however, is that students often graduate seminary with a smorgasbord of various methodologies and commitments, some of which may compete with one another. For example, a graduating student may claim to be simultaneously committed to a Wesleyan, charismatic, womanist theology aimed at a second-generation, evangelical Filipino American context but does not know how to integrate these contexts and convictions in a holistic manner. It is one thing to evaluate a student's biblical interpretation at the beginning of their studies when they are theological novices. It is a different task to do so after they have acquired many additional theological influences and have reflected on their sociocultural and ministry contexts.

At present, seminary students may be exposed to diverse perspectives throughout their studies but are given very little instruction on how to integrate their contexts with their theological commitments. Adding diverse readings to syllabi is important, but that alone does not teach students how to interpret the Bible theologically and contextually. More than reading lists need to be changed to accomplish this outcome; the very task of biblical interpretation needs to be redefined.

I have identified four competencies that are necessary to engage in theological and contextual biblical interpretation.

1. Reading or exegetical skills. I continue to use the term "exegesis" for close readings of the ancient biblical text. While there is a spectrum of views on the importance of exegesis among contextual and theological interpreters, they all value its contribution since this is *biblical* interpretation after all. In addition, I assume a theology of Scripture based on the contributions of theological interpretation.

2. Sociocultural reflection. Theology is always embodied and contextual, so interpreters must be self-aware and self-reflective as they read Scripture. In my classes I have employed a modified form of Norman Gottwald's self-inventory of the biblical interpreter from his "Framing Biblical Interpretation,"[1] with the hope to create my own self-inventory in the future. Students also read examples of other self-inventories by contextual interpreters, often narrated in the form of autobiography.

3. Theological, ethical, and ministerial commitments. I share my theological, ethical, and ministerial commitments with my students. I ask students to identify their own commitments to these three categories and to reflect on why they hold these commitments. Their values often reflect those of the ecclesial and sociocultural communities in which they participate.

4. Spiritual practices. Biblical interpretation, application, and proclamation are spiritual activities that require meditation, prayer, and discernment. Biblical interpretation involves making interpretive

1. Gottwald, "Framing Biblical Interpretation," 256–60.

connections and decisions, and interpreters inevitably have to prioritize one line of inquiry over others in their study. Meditation is the act of making connections between the biblical text and life, and prayer is required for wise interpretive discernment. Students report to me that writing their final paper caused them to do a lot of soul searching, and this confirms for me that biblical interpretation is an intense spiritual exercise.

When students write their final papers on theological and contextual interpretation, I ask them to describe how their contexts and theology shape their interpretation of the text. What theological and contextual interpretation requires of students is integrating these commitments and practices into a coherent whole. At times they will run into tensions or conflicts between the text, their theology, and their context. Theological and contextual interpretation is the act of negotiating these tensions for the sake of effective Christian ministry.

My course, Theological and Contextual Readings of the Old Testament, covers the following material:

1. Context of biblical studies. I expose students to premodern, modern, and postmodern approaches to Scripture. We cover the rise of historical criticism, its many forms, its assumptions, fundamentalist reactions to it, and then the move toward literary criticism, social-scientific criticism, and theological interpretation. We discuss the change in focus from texts to readers, and the proliferation of contextual interpretations.

2. Liberationist and postcolonial approaches. We start with classic liberation theology and hermeneutics and discuss critiques of it from various sectors. We discuss other liberationist approaches, such as African American and womanist forms, and we define postcolonial approaches and how they overlap and differ from liberationist approaches.

3. Global evangelical approaches. We discuss the explosion of global Christianity in the twentieth and twenty-first centuries, as well as its impact on theology. We learn from Lamin Sanneh and Andrew Walls on the central task of translating the gospel for a multicultural church; Kwame Bediako on the theological

importance of cultural identity; K. K. Yeo on cross-cultural interpretation; and Renie Choy on the impact of colonialism within global Christianity.

4. Texts or topics of Exodus, Isaiah, exile, and migration from a variety of approaches. Students read examples of interpreters integrating biblical exegesis, their sociocultural context, and their theological commitments with regard to these biblical texts and themes.

5. A framework to evaluate multicultural interpretation. We use Love Sechrest's book *Race & Rhyme* as a framework for theological and contextual interpretation based on the figural interpretation of Scripture. This framework serves as a rubric to evaluate theological and contextual interpretations of biblical texts. I offer a couple examples of my own theological and contextual interpretation and ask the students to evaluate whether I meet the established criteria.

For their final papers, students choose a passage, describe their context and theological commitments, and study the text to examine whether it addresses their contextual needs and to determine the degree to which its teaching does not align with their theological and ministerial interests. They describe how the biblical text, their sociocultural context, and their theological commitments influence their interpretive conclusions. Through this exercise, students practice theological and contextual interpretation for their own communities and critically reflect on the interpretive process.

BIBLIOGRAPHY

Abraham, William J., Jason E. Vickers, and Natalie B. Van Kirk, eds. *Canonical Theism: A Proposal for Theology and the Church*. Eerdmans, 2008.

Althaus-Reid, Marcella María. "Gustavo Gutiérrez Goes to Disneyland: Theme Park Theologies and the Diaspora of the Discourse of the Popular Theologian in Liberation Theology." In *Interpreting Beyond Borders*, edited by Fernando F. Segovia. Sheffield Academic, 2000.

Auerbach, Erich. "Figura." In *Scenes from the Drama of European Literature*, edited by Erich Auerbach. Meridian Books, 1959.

Bailey, Kenneth E. *Poet & Peasant and Through Peasant Eyes: A Literary-Cultural Approach to the Parables in Luke*. Eerdmans, 1983.

Bartholomew, Craig G. Introduction to *Renewing Biblical Interpretation*, edited by Craig Bartholomew, Colin Greene, and Karl Moller. Zondervan, 2000.

Bartholomew, Craig G., and Heath A. Thomas, eds. *A Manifesto for Theological Interpretation*. Baker Academic, 2016.

Barton, John. *The Nature of Biblical Criticism*. Westminster John Knox, 2007.

Bediako, Kwame. "Biblical Exegesis in the African Context: The Factor and Impact of Translated Scriptures." *Journal of African Christian Thought* 6 (2003): 15–23.

———. *Jesus and the Gospel in Africa: History and Experience*. Orbis Books, 2004.

———. *Theology and Identity: The Impact of Culture upon Christian Thought in the Second Century and in Modern Africa.* Regnum Press International, 1999.

Bevans, Stephen B. *Models of Contextual Theology.* Rev. and expanded ed. Orbis Books, 2002.

Bloom, Harold. *The Western Canon: The Books and School of the Ages.* Macmillan, 1994.

Blount, Brian K. *Cultural Interpretation: Reorienting New Testament Interpretation.* Augsburg Fortress, 1995.

Boff, Leonardo, and Clodovis Boff. *Introducing Liberation Theology.* Translated by Paul Burns. Orbis Books, 1987.

Bowens, Lisa M. *African American Readings of Paul: Reception, Resistance, and Transformation.* Eerdmans, 2020.

Branson, Mark Lau, and C. René Padilla, eds. *Conflict and Context: Hermeneutics in the Americas.* Eerdmans, 1986.

Brett, Mark G. *Decolonizing God: The Bible in the Tides of Empire.* The Bible in the Modern World 16. Sheffield Phoenix, 2008.

———. *Political Trauma and Healing: Biblical Ethics for a Postcolonial World.* Eerdmans, 2016.

Briggs, Richard S. *The Virtuous Reader: Old Testament Narrative and Interpretive Virtue.* Studies in Theological Interpretation. Baker Academic, 2010.

Brueggemann, Walter. "Pharoah as Vassal: A Study of a Political Metaphor." *Catholic Biblical Quarterly* 57 (1995): 27–51.

Cardenal, Ernesto. *Love in Practice: The Gospel in Solentiname.* Translated by Donald D. Walsh. Search, 1977.

Carey, Greg. *Using Our Outside Voice: Public Biblical Interpretation.* Fortress, 2020.

Carroll, Robert P. "An Infinity of Traces: On Making an Inventory of Our Ideological Holdings. An Introduction to Ideologiekritik in Biblical Studies." *Journal of Northwest Semitic Languages* 21 (1995): 25–43.

Carter, J. Kameron. *Race: A Theological Account.* Oxford University Press, 2008.

Chan, Simon. *Grassroots Asian Theology: Thinking the Faith from the Ground Up.* InterVarsity, 2014.

Childs, Brevard S. *The Book of Exodus: A Critical, Theological Commentary.* Old Testament Library. Westminster, 1974.

———. *Introduction to the Old Testament as Scripture.* Fortress, 1979.

———. *Isaiah.* Old Testament Library. Westminster John Knox, 2001.

———. *The Struggle to Understand Isaiah as Christian Scripture.* Eerdmans, 2004.

Choy, Renie Chow. *Ancestral Feeling: Postcolonial Thoughts on Western Christian Heritage.* SCM, 2021.

Clements, Ronald E. *A Century of Old Testament Study.* Lutterworth, 1976.

Clifford, Hywel, Douglas Earl, Ryan P. O'Dowd, and Lena-Sofia Tiemeyer. *Companion to the Old Testament: Introduction, Interpretation, Application.* SCM, 2016.

Coakley, Sarah. *God, Sexuality, and the Self: An Essay 'On the Trinity.'* Cambridge University Press, 2013.

Coffey, John. Introduction to *The Post-Reformation Era 1559–1689*, edited by John Coffey. Vol. 1 of *The Oxford History of Protestant Dissenting Traditions.* Oxford University Press, 2020.

Collett, Don C. *Figural Reading and the Old Testament: Theology and Practice.* Baker Academic, 2020.

Collins, John J. *The Bible After Babel: Historical Criticism in a Postmodern Age.* Eerdmans, 2005.

Conde-Frazier, Elizabeth. *Atando Cabos: Latinx Contributions to Theological Education.* Theological Education Between the Times. Eerdmans, 2021.

Cosgrove, Charles H., Herold Weiss, and Khiok-khng Yeo. *Cross-Cultural Paul: Journeys to Others, Journeys to Ourselves.* Eerdmans, 2005.

Cuéllar, Gregory L. *Empire, the British Museum, and the Making of the Biblical Scholar in the Nineteenth Century.* Palgrave Macmillan, 2019.

Davis, Ellen F., and Richard B. Hays, eds. *The Art of Reading Scripture.* Eerdmans, 2003.

Dawson, John David. *Christian Figural Reading and the Fashioning of Identity.* University of California Press, 2002.

Day, Keri. *Notes of a Native Daughter: Testifying in Theological Education.* Theological Education Between the Times. Eerdmans, 2021.

Day, Linda, and Carolyn Pressler, eds. *Engaging the Bible in a Gendered World: An Introduction to Feminist Biblical Interpretation in Honor of Katharine Doob Sakenfeld.* Westminster John Knox, 2006.

de Wit, Hans. "Exegesis and Contextuality: Happy Marriage, Divorce, or Living (Apart) Together?" In *African and European Readers of the Bible in Dialogue: In Quest of a Shared Meaning*, edited by Hans de Wit and Gerald O. West. Brill, 2008.

de Wit, Hans, Hans Snoek, and Gerald O. West. Introduction to *African and European Readers of the Bible in Dialogue: In Quest of a Shared Meaning*, edited by Hans de Wit and Gerald O. West. Brill, 2008.

Dietrich, Walter, and Ulrich Luz, eds. *The Bible in a World Context: An Experiment in Contextual Hermeneutics*. Eerdmans, 2002.

Dyrness, William A., and Veli-Matti Kärkkäinen, eds. *Global Dicionary of Theology*. InterVarsity, 2008.

East, Brad. *The Church's Book: Theology of Scripture in Ecclesial Context*. Eerdmans, 2022.

Ekblad, Bob. *Reading the Bible with the Damned*. Westminster John Knox, 2005.

Foskett, Mary F., and Jeffrey Kah-Jin Kuan, eds. *Ways of Being, Ways of Reading: Asian American Biblical Interpretation*. Chalice, 2006.

Foucault, Michel. "The Subject and Power." In *Essential Works of Foucault*, edited by James D. Faubion. New Press, 1994.

Fowl, Stephen E. *Engaging Scripture: A Model for Theological Interpretation*. Challenges in Contemporary Theology. Blackwell, 1998.

———. *Theological Interpretation of Scripture*. Cascade Companions. Cascade Books, 2009.

Fowl, Stephen E., and L. Gregory Jones. *Reading in Communion: Scripture and Ethics in Christian Life*. Eerdmans, 1991.

Frei, Hans W. *The Eclipse of Biblical Narrative: A Study in Eighteenth and Nineteenth Century Hermeneutics*. Yale University Press, 1974.

Fretheim, Sara J. *Kwame Bediako and African Christian Scholarship: Emerging Religious Discourse in Twentieth-Century Ghana*. Pickwick, 2018.

Gnonhossou, Sègbégnon M. "Who Were the Enslaved?" Seattle Pacific University Walls Lecture, April 25, 2023.

Goheen, Michael W., ed. *Reading the Bible Missionally*. The Gospel and Our Culture Series. Eerdmans, 2016.

González, Justo L. *Santa Biblia: The Bible Through Hispanic Eyes*. Abingdon, 1996.

Gorman, Michael J., ed. *Elements of Biblical Exegesis: A Basic Guide for Students and Ministers*. 3rd ed. Baker Academic, 2020.

———. *Scripture: An Ecumenical Introduction to the Bible and Its Interpretation*. Hendrickson, 2005.

———, ed. *Scripture and Its Interpretation: A Global, Ecumenical Introduction to the Bible.* Baker Academic, 2017.

Gornik, Mark R. *Word Made Global: Stories of African Christianity in New York City.* Eerdmans, 2011.

Goto, Courtney T. *Taking on Practical Theology: The Idolization of Context and the Hope of Community.* Theology in Practice 6. Brill, 2018.

Gottwald, Norman K. "Framing Biblical Interpretation." In Segovia and Tolbert, *Readings from This Place.*

Gramsci, Antonio. *Selections from the Prison Notebooks of Antonio Gramsci.* International Publishers, 1973.

Granberg-Michaelson, Wesley. *Future Faith: Ten Challenges Reshaping Christianity in the 21st Century.* Fortress, 2018.

Green, Gene L., Stephen T. Pardue, and K. K. Yeo, eds. *Majority World Theology: Christian Doctrine in Global Context.* IVP Academic, 2020.

Green, Joel B. "A Discursive Frame for Reading Scripture." In *Acts of Interpretation: Scripture, Theology, and Culture*, edited by Stephen A. Cummins and Jens Zimmermann. Eerdmans, 2018.

———. *Practicing Theological Interpretation: Engaging Biblical Texts for Faith and Formation.* Baker Academic, 2011.

Greene-McCreight, Kathryn. "Rule of Faith." In Vanhoozer, *Dictionary for Theological Interpretation.*

Greenfield-Sanders, Timothy, dir. *Toni Morrison: The Pieces I Am.* Perfect Day Films, 2019.

Gutiérrez, Gustavo. *The God of Life.* Translated by Matthew J. O'Connell. Orbis Books, 1991.

———. *On Job: God-Talk and the Suffering of the Innocent.* Translated by Matthew J. O'Connell. Orbis Books, 1987.

———. *A Theology of Liberation: History, Politics, and Salvation.* Translated by Caridad Inda and John Eagleson. Rev. ed. SCM, 1988.

———. *We Drink from Our Own Wells: The Spiritual Journey of a People.* Orbis Books, 1984.

Harris, Michael S. *Understanding Institutional Diversity in American Higher Education.* ASHE Higher Education Report 39.3. Wiley Periodicals, 2013.

Hart, David Bentley. *Tradition and Apocalypse: An Essay on the Future of Christian Belief.* Baker Academic, 2022.

Hartman, Tim. *Kwame Bediako: African Theology for a World Christianity.* Langham Global Library, 2021.

———. *Theology After Colonization: Bediako, Barth, and the Future of Theological Reflection*. University of Notre Dame Press, 2019.

Hayes, John H., and Carl R. Holladay. *Biblical Exegesis: A Beginner's Handbook*. John Knox, 1982.

———. *Biblical Exegesis: A Beginner's Handbook*. 3rd ed. Westminster John Knox, 2007.

Hays, Richard B. *The Moral Vision of the New Testament: Community, Cross, New Creation: A Contemporary Introduction to New Testament Ethics*. HarperOne, 1996.

———. "Reading the Bible with Eyes of Faith: The Practice of Theological Exegesis." *Journal of Theological Interpretation* 1.1 (2007): 5–21.

Heaney, Sharon E. *Contextual Theology for Latin America: Liberation Themes in Evangelical Perspective*. Paternoster Theological Monographs. Paternoster, 2008.

Hertig, Young Lee, and Chloe Sun, eds. *Mirrored Reflections: Reframing Biblical Characters*. Wipf & Stock, 2010.

Holland, Frederic May. *Frederick Douglass: The Colored Orator*. Funk & Wagnalls, 1895.

Janzen, David. *The Liberation of Method: The Ethics of Emancipatory Biblical Interpretation*. Fortress, 2021.

Jenkins, Philip. *The New Faces of Christianity: Believing the Bible in the Global South*. Oxford University Press, 2006.

Jennings, Willie James. *After Whiteness: An Education in Belonging*. Theological Education Between the Times. Eerdmans, 2020.

———. *The Christian Imagination: Theology and the Origins of Race*. Yale University Press, 2010.

Jenson, Robert W. "The Religious Power of Scripture." *Scottish Journal of Theology* 52 (1999): 89–105.

John, T. K. "Two Narratives: Judeo-Christian and Indic Enslavement and Liberation." In *One Volume Dalit Bible Commentary: Old Testament*, edited by James Massey. Centre for Dalit Subaltern Studies, 2015.

Kamudzandu, Israel. *Abraham as Spiritual Ancestor: A Postcolonial Zimbabwean Reading of Romans 4*. Brill, 2010.

Kelsey, David H. *The Uses of Scripture in Recent Theology*. Fortress, 1975.

Kim, Chan-Hie. "Reading the Cornelius Story from an Asian Immigrant Perspective." In Segovia and Tolbert, *Reading from This Place*.

Kim, Grace Ji-Sun. *Embracing the Other: The Transformative Spirit of Love.* Prophetic Christianity. Eerdmans, 2015.

Kim, Jean K. "Empowerment or Enslavement?: Reading John 4 Intertextually with Ezra-Nehemiah." In Foskett and Kuan, *Ways of Being.*

Kim, Uriah Y. "Uriah the Hittite: A Con(text) of Struggle for Identity." *Semeia* 90–91 (2002): 69–85.

Kirkpatrick, David C. *A Gospel for the Poor: Global Social Christianity and the Latin American Evangelical Left.* University of Pennsylvania Press, 2019.

Kwok, Pui-lan. "Finding Ruth a Home: Gender, Sexuality, and the Politics of Otherness." In *Postcolonial Imagination and Feminist Theology.* Westminster John Knox, 2005.

Lee, Eunny P. "Ruth the Moabite: Identity, Kinship, and Otherness." In Day and Pressler, *Engaging the Bible.*

Levenson, Jon D. *The Hebrew Bible, the Old Testament, and Historical Criticism.* Westminster John Knox, 1993.

Lim, Bo H. "Critical Methods and Critiques: Theological Interpretation." In *T&T Clark Handbook of Asian American Biblical Hermeneutics,* edited by Uriah Kim and Seung Ai Yang. T&T Clark, 2019.

———. "Reading in Context." In *The State of Old Testament Studies,* edited by H. H. Hardy and M. Daniel Carroll R. Baker Academic, 2024.

———. "The Task of Reading the Bible for a Culturally Diverse North American Church." In *The Scripture and Hermeneutics Seminar: Retrospect and Prospect,* edited by Craig G. Bartholomew, David J. H. Beldman, Amber Bowen, and William Olhausen. Zondervan, 2022.

Lim, Bo H., and Daniel Castelo. *Hosea.* Two Horizons Old Testament Commentary. Eerdmans, 2015.

Lim, Timothy H. "How Good Was Ruth's Hebrew? Ethnic and Linguistic Otherness in the Book of Ruth." In *The "Other" in Second Temple Judaism: Essays in Honor of John J. Collins,* edited by Daniel C. Harlow, Karina Martin Hogan, Matthew Goff, and Joel S. Kaminsky. Eerdmans, 2011.

Lindbeck, George A. *The Nature of Doctrine: Religion and Theology in a Postliberal Age.* Westminster, 1984.

Loewen, Jacob A. *The Bible in Cross-Cultural Perspective.* William Carey Library, 2000.

MacIntyre, Alasdair. *After Virtue: A Study in Moral Theory.* University of Notre Dame Press, 1984.

———. *Whose Justice? Which Rationality?* University of Notre Dame Press, 1988.

Marsh, Charles. *The Beloved Community: How Faith Shapes Social Justice from the Civil Rights Movement to Today.* Basic Books, 2005.

———. Introduction to *Lived Theology: New Perspectives on Method, Style, and Pedagogy,* edited by Charles Marsh, Peter Slade, and Sarah Azaransky. Oxford University Press, 2017.

Martin, Dale B. *Pedagogy of the Bible: An Analysis and Proposal.* Westminster John Knox, 2008.

Mbiti, John S. "African Indigenous Culture in Relation to Evangelism and Church Development." In *The Gospel and Frontier Peoples,* edited by R. Pierce Beaver. William Carey Library, 1973.

———. *African Religions and Philosophy.* Heinemann, 1969.

———. *Bible and Theology in African Christianity.* Oxford University Press, 1986.

———. "Some African Concepts of Christology." In *Christ and the Younger Churches,* edited by Georg F. Vicedom. SPCK, 1972.

Mburu, Elizabeth. *African Hermeneutics.* Hippo Books, 2019.

Moberly, R. W. L. *The Bible, Theology, and Faith: A Study of Abraham and Jesus.* Cambridge Studies in Christian Doctrine. Cambridge University Press, 2000.

———. "What Is Theological Interpretation of Scripture?" *Journal of Theological Interpretation* 3.2 (2009): 161–78.

Moore, Stephen D., and Yvonne Sherwood. *The Invention of the Biblical Scholar: A Critical Manifesto.* Fortress, 2011.

Moy, Russell G. "Resident Aliens of the Diaspora: 1 Peter and Chinese Protestants in San Francisco." In *The Bible in Asian America,* edited by Tatsiong Benny Liew and Gale A. Yee. Society of Biblical Literature, 2002.

Müller, Mogens. *The First Bible of the Church: A Plea for the Septuagint.* Journal for the Study of the Old Testament: Supplement Series 206. Sheffield Academic, 1996.

Ngan, Lai Ling Elizabeth. "Neither Here nor There: Boundary and Identity in the Hagar Story." In Foskett and Kuan, *Ways of Being.*

Ochs, Peter, ed. *The Return to Scripture: Essays in Postcritical Scriptural Interpretation.* Paulist, 1993.

O'Day, Gail R., and David L. Petersen, eds. *Theological Bible Commentary.* Westminster John Knox, 2009.

Ott, Craig, and Harold A. Netland, eds. *Globalizing Theology: Belief and Practice in an Era of World Christianity.* Apollos, 2007.

Pa, Anna May Say. "Reading Ruth 3:1–5 from an Asian Woman's Perspective." In Day and Pressler, *Engaging the Bible.*

Paddison, Angus. "The History and Reemergence of Theological Interpretation." In Bartholomew and Thomas, *Manifesto for Theological Interpretation.*

Parker, Angela N. *If God Still Breathes, Why Can't I?: Black Lives Matter and Biblical Authority.* Eerdmans, 2021.

Patte, Daniel. "Acknowledging the Contextual Character of Male, European-American Critical Exegesis: An Androcritical Perspective." In Segovia and Tolberts, *Readings from This Place.*

———. "The Guarded Personal Voice of a Male European-American Biblical Scholar." In *The Personal Voice in Biblical Interpretation,* edited by Ingrid Rosa Kitzberger. Routledge, 1998.

———. Introduction to *Global Bible Interpretation,* edited by Daniel Patte. Abingdon, 1994.

Penner, Todd, and Davina C. Lopez. *De-Introducing the New Testament: Texts, Worlds, Methods, Stories.* Wiley Blackwell, 2015.

Perdue, Leo G. *The Collapse of History: Reconstructing Old Testament Theology.* Overtures to Biblical Theology. Fortress, 1994.

———. *Reconstructing Old Testament Theology: After the Collapse of History.* Overtures to Biblical Theology. Fortress, 2005.

Placher, William C. *Mark.* Belief: A Theological Commentary on the Bible. Westminster John Knox, 2010.

Placher, William C., and Amy Plantinga Pauw. Series Introduction to *Mark,* by William C. Placher. Belief: A Theological Commentary on the Bible. Westminster John Knox, 2010.

Pope-Levison, Priscilla, and John R. Levison, eds. *Return to Babel: Global Perspectives on the Bible.* Westminster John Knox, 1999.

Powery, Emerson B., and Rodney Steven Sadler. *The Genesis of Liberation: Biblical Interpretation in the Antebellum Narratives of the Enslaved.* Westminster John Knox, 2016.

Radner, Ephraim. *Time and the Word: Figural Reading of the Christian Scriptures.* Eerdmans, 2016.

Räisänen, Heikki. *Beyond New Testament Theology: A Story and a Programme*. 2nd ed. SCM, 2000.

Rietz, Henry W. Morisada. "A Hapa Identifying with the Exodus, the Exile, and the Internment." In Foskett and Kuan, *Ways of Being*.

Romero, Robert Chao. *Brown Church: Five Centuries of Latina/o Social Justice, Theology, and Identity*. InterVarsity, 2020.

Salinas, Daniel. *Latin American Evangelical Theology in the 1970's: The Golden Decade*. Religion in the Americas Series 9. Brill, 2009.

Sanneh, Lamin. *Translating the Message: The Missionary Impact on Culture*. Orbis Books, 1989.

———. *Whose Religion Is Christianity? The Gospel Beyond the West*. Eerdmans, 2003.

Sarisky, Darren. *Reading the Bible Theologically*. Current Issues in Theology. Cambridge University Press, 2019.

Sechrest, Love Lazarus. *Race & Rhyme: Rereading the New Testament*. Eerdmans, 2022.

Segovia, Fernando F. "Intercultural Bible Reading as Transformation for Liberation: Intercultural Hermeneutics and Biblical Studies." In *Bible and Transformation: The Promise of Intercultural Bible Reading*, edited by Hans de Wit and Janet Dyk. SBL Press, 2015.

———. "Interpreting Beyond Borders: Postcolonial Studies and Diasporic Studies in Biblical Criticism." In *Interpreting Beyond Borders*, edited by Fernando R. Segovia. Sheffield Academic, 2000.

———. "Introduction: Approaching Latino/a Biblical Criticism: A Trajectory of Visions and Missions." In *Latino/a Biblical Hermeneutics: Problematics, Objectives, Strategies*, edited by Francisco Lozada Jr. and Fernando F. Segovia. SBL Press, 2014.

———. "Toward a Hermeneutics of Diaspora: A Hermeneutics of Otherness and Engagement." In Segovia and Tolbert, *Readings from This Place*.

Segovia, Fernando F., and Mary Ann Tolbert, eds. *Readings from This Place*. Vol. 1, *Social Location and Biblical Interpretation in the United States*. Fortress, 1995.

Seitz, Christopher R., ed. *Nicene Christianity: The Future for a New Ecumenism*. Brazos, 2001.

Smart, James D. *The Strange Silence of the Bible in the Church: A Study in Hermeneutics*. Westminster, 1970.

Steinmetz, David C. "The Superiority of Pre-Critical Exegesis." *Theology Today* 37 (1980): 27–38.

Sugirtharajah, R. S. *Asian Biblical Hermeneutics and Postcolonialism: Contesting the Interpretations*. Orbis Books, 1998.

———. "Muddling Along at the Margins." In *Still at the Margins: Biblical Scholarship Fifteen Years After Voices from the Margin*, edited by R. S. Sugirtharajah. T&T Clark, 2008.

———. *Postcolonial Criticism and Biblical Interpretation*. Oxford University Press, 2002.

———. *Troublesome Texts: The Bible in Colonial and Contemporary Culture*. Sheffield Phoenix, 2008.

Sun, Chloe Tse. *Attempt Great Things for God: Theological Education in Diaspora*. Theological Education Between the Times. Eerdmans, 2020.

Swete, Henry Barclay. *An Introduction to the Old Testament in Greek*. Cambridge University Press, 1914.

Tamez, Elsa. *The Amnesty of Grace: Justification by Faith from a Latin American Perspective*. Translated by S. H. Ringe. Abingdon, 1993.

Tanner, Kathryn. *Theories of Culture: A New Agenda for Theology*. Guides to Theological Inquiry. Fortress, 1997.

Thiselton, Anthony J. "The Future of Biblical Interpretation and Responsible Plurality in Hermeneutics." In *The Future of Biblical Interpretation: Responsible Plurality in Biblical Hermeneutics*, edited by Stanley E. Porter and Matthew R. Malcolm. InterVarsity, 2013.

Thompson, John L. *Reading the Bible with the Dead*. Eerdmans, 2007.

Thurman, Howard. *Jesus and the Disinherited*. Beacon, 1996.

Tran, Jonathan. *Asian Americans and the Spirit of Racial Capitalism*. Oxford University Press, 2020.

Treier, Daniel J. *Introducing Theological Interpretation of Scripture: Recovering a Christian Practice*. Baker Academic, 2008.

Ukpong, Justin. "Inculturation Hermeneutics: An African Approach to Biblical Interpretation." In Dietrich and Luz, *Bible in a World Context*.

Van Engen, Charles E. "The Glocal Church: Locality and Catholicity in a Globalizing World." In Ott and Netland, *Globalizing Theology*.

Vanhoozer, Kevin J., ed. *Dictionary for Theological Interpretation of the Bible*. Baker Academic, 2005.

———. "Introduction: What Is Theological Interpretation of the Bible?" In Vanhoozer, *Dictionary for Theological Interpretation*.

Walls, Andrew F. "Globalization and the Study of Christian History." In Ott and Netland, *Globalizing Theology*.

―――. *The Missionary Movement in Christian history: Studies in the Transmission of Faith*. Orbis Books, 1996.

Watson, Francis. *Text, Church and World: Biblical Interpretation in Theological Perspective*. Eerdmans, 1994.

Webster, John. *Holy Scripture: A Dogmatic Sketch*. Current Issues in Theology. Cambridge University Press, 2003.

―――. "Theologies of Retrieval." In *The Oxford Handbook of Systematic Theology*, edited by John Webster, Kathryn Tanner, and Iain R. Torrance. Oxford University Press, 2007.

Weems, Renita J. "Re-Reading for Liberation: African American Women and the Bible, 25th Anniversary Edition." In *Voices from the Margin: Interpreting the Bible in the Third World*, edited by R. S. Sugirtharajah. Orbis Books, 2016.

Wesley, John. *The Doctrine of Original Sin According to Scripture, Reason, and Experience*. Bristol, 1757.

―――. *Thoughts upon Slavery*. London, 1774.

West, Cornel. *Prophesy Deliverance!: An Afro-American Revolutionary Christianity*. Westminster, 1982.

West, Gerald O. *Biblical Hermeneutics of Liberation*. Cluster, 1991.

―――, ed. *Reading Other-Wise: Socially Engaged Biblical Scholars Reading with Their Local Communities*. Society of Biblical Literature, 2007.

Winner, Lauren F. *The Dangers of Christian Practice: On Wayward Gifts, Characteristic Damage, and Sin*. Yale University Press, 2018.

Wolterstorff, Nicholas. "The Travail of Theology in the Modern Academy." In *The Future of Theology: Essays in Honor of Jürgen Moltmann*, edited by Miroslav Volf, Carmen Krieg, and Thomas Dörken-Kucharz. Eerdmans, 1996.

Wrogemann, Henning. *Intercultural Theology*. Vol. 1, *Intercultural Hermeneutics*. Translated by Karl E. Böhmer. IVP Academic, 2016.

Yamada, Frank M. "What Does Manzanar Have to Do with Eden? A Japanese American Interpretation of Genesis 2–3." In *They Were All Together in One Place? Toward Minority Biblical Criticism*, edited by Randall C. Bailey, Tat-siong Benny Liew, and Fernando F. Segovia. Society of Biblical Literature, 2009.

Yee, Gale A. "'She Stood in Tears amid the Alien Corn': Ruth, the Perpetual Foreigner and Model Minority." In *Off the Menu: Asian and Asian North American Women's Religion and Theology*, edited by Rita Nakashima

Brock, Jung Ha Kim, Pui-lan Kwok, and Seung Ai Yang. Westminster John Knox, 2007.

Yeh, Allen, and Tite Tiénou, eds. *Majority World Theologies: Theologizing from Africa, Asia, Latin America, and the Ends of the Earth.* William Carey, 2018.

Yeo, Khiok-khng (K. K.). "Biblical Christologies of the Global Church: Beyond Chalcedon? Toward a Fully Christian and Fully Cultural Theology." In Green, Pardue, and Yeo, *Majority World Theology.*

———. *Chairman Mao Meets the Apostle Paul: Christianity, Communism, and the Hope of China.* Brazos, 2002.

———. "Culture and Intersubjectivity as Criteria for Negotiating Meanings in Cross-Cultural Interpretations." In *The Meanings We Choose: Hermeneutical Ethics, Indeterminacy and the Conflict of Interpretations,* edited by Charles Cosgrove. Journal for the Study of the Old Testament: Supplement Series 411. T&T Clark, 2004.

———. *Musing with Confucius and Paul: Toward a Chinese Christian Theology.* Cascade Books, 2008.

———, ed. *The Oxford Handbook of the Bible in China.* Oxford University Press, 2021.

———. "Response: Multicultural Readings: A Biblical Warrant and an Eschatological Vision." In *Global Voices: Reading the Bible in the Majority World,* edited by Craig S. Keener and M. Daniel Carroll R. Hendrickson, 2013.

———. *Rhetorical Interaction in 1 Corinthians 8 and 10: A Formal Analysis with Preliminary Suggestions for a Chinese, Cross-Cultural Hermeneutic.* Biblical Interpretation Series 9. Brill, 1995.

———. *What Has Jerusalem to Do with Beijing? Biblical Interpretation from a Chinese Perspective.* 2nd ed. Pickwick, 2018.

Yong, Amos. *Renewing the Church by the Spirit: Theological Education After Pentecost.* Theological Education Between the Times. Eerdmans, 2020.

AUTHOR INDEX